THREE PLAYS

THREE PLAYS

ESCAPE : THE ELDEST SON : THE SKIN GAME

JOHN GALSWORTHY

PAN BOOKS LTD   LONDON

These plays first published by Gerald Duckworth & Co., Ltd.
("Escape" 1926, "The Eldest Son" 1912, "The Skin Game" 1920)
This edition published 1948 by Pan Books Ltd.
8 Headfort Place, London, S.W.1

CONTENTS

	PAGE
ESCAPE	7
THE ELDEST SON	73
THE SKIN GAME	133

ESCAPE

CAST OF THE ORIGINAL PRODUCTION AT THE AMBASSADORS THEATRE, LONDON, AUGUST 12, 1926

PRODUCED BY LEON M. LION

MATT DENANT	*Nicholas Hannen*
THE GIRL OF THE TOWN	*Ursula Jeans*
THE PLAIN CLOTHES MAN	*Frank Freeman*
THE POLICEMAN	*Harold Lester*
THE OTHER POLICEMAN	*Cyril Hardingham*
THE FELLOW CONVICT	*Leon M. Lion*
THE WARDER	*Gerard Clifton*
THE OTHER WARDER	*Stafford Hilliard*
THE SHINGLED LADY	*Molly Kerr*
THE MAID	*Phyllis Konstam*
THE OLD GENTLEMAN	*Leon M. Lion*
THE CAPTAIN	*Gerard Clifton*
THE SHOPKEEPER	*Paul Gill*
HIS WIFE	*Ethel Manning*
HIS SISTER	*Ann Codrington*
THE MAN IN PLUS FOURS	*Stafford Hilliard*
HIS WIFE	*Phyllis Konstam*
THE DARTMOOR CONSTABLE	*Frank Freeman*
THE LABOURER	*Cyril Hardingham*
THE OTHER LABOURER	*Harold Lester*
THE FARMER	*Paul Gill*
THE LITTLE GIRL	*Betty Astell*
MISS GRACE	*Ann Codrington*
MISS DORA	*Margaret Halstan*
THE PARSON	*Austin Trevor*
THE BELLRINGER	*Stafford Hilliard*

PROLOGUE

Hyde Park at night. Summer. The Row with its iron railing, footwalk, seats, trees and bushes behind. A WOMAN, or GIRL (you can't tell), is sitting alone, in dim radiance from lamps unseen to Right and Left. Her painted mask is not unattractive, her attitude slack and uneasy. A PLAIN CLOTHES MAN passes Right to Left, glances at her inviting him and increases his pace. By the expression on her face as he approaches and recedes, it is easy for him to see what she is. TWO PEOPLE pass without glancing at her at all—they are talking of what "he said to me" and "I said to him." Then nobody passes, and, powdering her nose, she seems preparing to shift along, when from the Left, MATT DENANT appears strolling. He is a young man, tallish and athletic, dressed as if he has been racing in hot weather; he has a pair of race glasses and a cigar. The GIRL shifts forward on her seat as he approaches. He is going by when she looks suddenly up and says in a low voice: "Good evening!" He halts, looks at her, gives a little shrug, carries his hand to his hat, and answering, "Good evening!" is moving on when she speaks again.

GIRL. Have you a match? [*She is holding out a cigarette; he stops and hands her his cigarette lighter.*]

GIRL. [*Fingering the lighter*] Gold?

MATT. Brass.

GIRL. Have one? [*Offering her cigarette case.*

MATT. Thanks, I'm smoking. [*He shows her his cigar; resting his foot on the seat and dangling his race glasses.*]

GIRL. Been racing?

MATT. Goodwood.

9

GIRL. I went to see the Jubilee this year.

MATT. And what did you back?

GIRL. Everything that didn't win. It's rotten when you don't back winners.

MATT. Don't you like the horses?

GIRL. They look pretty.

MATT. Prettiest things in the world.

GIRL. Pretty as women?

MATT. Saving your presence.

GIRL. Do you mean that?

MATT. Well, you get a woman once in a way that can arch her neck.

GIRL. You don't like women—that's clear.

MATT. Not too much.

GIRL. [Smiling] You speak your mind, anyway.

MATT. If you ask me, they've got such a lot of vice about 'em compared with horses.

GIRL. And who puts vice into them?

MATT. I know—you all say men, but d'you believe it?

GIRL. [With a laugh] Well, I don't know. Don't men put vice into horses?

MATT. [Struck] M'yes! [Sitting down.] All the same, there's nothing wilder than a wild horse—I've seen 'em out West.

GIRL. There's nothing so wild as a wild woman.

[A momentary silence while they stare at each other.

MATT. Women haven't the excuse of horses—they've been tame since Eve gave Adam his tea.

GIRL. Um! Garden of Eden! Must have been something like Hyde Park—there was a prize cop there, anyway.

MATT. D'you come here often?

GIRL. [Nodding] Where else can one go? They're so particular now.

MATT. They do seem to keep you on the run.

GIRL. What are you—soldier?

MATT. Once upon a time.

GIRL. What now?

MATT. Thinking of being a parson.

GIRL. [*Laughs*] You've got money of your own, then?

MATT. A little.

GIRL. [*With a sigh*] If I had money of my own, d'you know what I'd do?

MATT. Get rid of it.

GIRL. Just what I wouldn't. If ever I got myself dependent on you men again, [*Very grimly*] shut my lights off.

MATT. Not like the lady under laughing gas.

GIRL. What was the matter with her?

MATT. Kept shouting, "I don't want to be a free, independent, economic agent! I want to be loved."

GIRL. She was wrong—No, *sir!* Get my head under a second time? Not much! But we can't save—don't make enough. So there you are! It's a good bit worse than it used to be, they say——

MATT. The ordinary girl more free and easy now, you mean?

GIRL. [*Grimly*] The *ordinary* girl?

MATT. Well, you don't call yourself ordinary, do you?

[*The* GIRL *sits quite still and doesn't answer.*

MATT. Sorry! Didn't mean to hurt you.

GIRL. Give me the fellow that does: he doesn't hurt half so much. But you're quite right. [*Bitterly.*] There isn't much excuse for us, now.

MATT. Aren't we getting a bit solemn?

GIRL. The gay girl—eh? They say you get used to anything: but I'll tell you—you never get used to playing the canary when you don't feel like it.

MATT. Ah! I always sympathized with canaries—expected to sing, and so permanently yellow.

GIRL. It was nice of you to sit down and talk.

MATT. Thanks; it's all secondary education.

[*She slides her hand along to his, with a card.*

GIRL. Here's my address; you might come and see me now and then.

MATT. [*Twiddling the card—amused and embarrassed*] On verra !

GIRL. What's that?

MATT. It's an expression of hope.

GIRL. [*Mouth opening*] Ow! How about now?

MATT. Thanks—afraid not—due somewhere at ten.

GIRL. Another?

MATT. No.

GIRL. You don't like me, I believe.

MATT. [*With a shrug*] Oh! Don't say that. You're original.

GIRL. Original sin.

MATT. There are worse things, I guess.

GIRL. You bet! There's modest worth. If *that* isn't worse! Not that this is a pretty life. It's just about as rotten as it can be.

MATT. How did you get into it?

GIRL. Cut it out! You all ask that, and you can take it from me you never get told. Well! I belong to the oldest profession in the world! That isn't true, either—there's an older.

MATT. Not really.

GIRL. The cop's. Mine wouldn't ever have been a profession but for them.

MATT. Good for you!

GIRL. It isn't good for me. Look in at Bow Street on Monday morning.

MATT. To see 'em shoot the sitting pheasant?—no, thanks. The Law isn't exactly sporting. Can't be, I suppose, if it's got to keep the course clear.

GIRL. They might wait till one makes oneself a nuisance.

MATT. Ever been run in?

GIRL. [*With a look, and a decision*] Um! Not yet!

[*Suddenly.*] What can we do? If we don't make a sign, who's to know us?

MATT. That's delightful.

GIRL. Clean streets!—that's the cry. Clean men! That'd be better!

MATT. And then where'd you be?

GIRL. [*Passionately*] Not here!

MATT. [*After staring at her*] Um! The kettle and the pot. What! Give me horses and dogs, all the time.

GIRL. I've got a cat.

MATT. Persian?

GIRL. [*Nodding*] A real beauty. [*Suddenly.*] Wouldn't you like to come and see him?

> [*He shakes his head, rises, takes his glasses, and holds out his hand. She is going to take it—then draws her hand back sharply, frowning and biting her lips. He gives a shrug, salutes, and moves on. She catches at his sleeve, misses it, sits a second, then rises and follows. Unseen by her, the* PLAIN CLOTHES MAN *has reappeared, Left. He moves swiftly and grasps her arm just as she is vanishing Right. The* GIRL *gives a little squeal as he draws her back towards the seat. She resists.*]

GIRL. Who are *you*?

PLAIN CLOTHES MAN. Plain clothes. [*And, as she still resists, he tries to calm her by a slight twist of the arm.*]

GIRL. You brute—you brute!

PLAIN CLOTHES MAN. Now then—quietly, and you won't get hurt.

GIRL. I wasn't doing anything.

PLAIN CLOTHES MAN. Oh! no, of course not.

GIRL. [*Looking after* MATT] I wasn't, I tell you; and he'll tell you so too! [MATT *has reappeared, Right.* Won't you? You talked to me of your own accord?

MATT. I did. Who may you be?

PLAIN CLOTHES MAN. [*Showing his card*] This woman accosted you. I've observed her carefully, and not for the first time.

MATT. Well, you've made a blooming error. We had a chat, that's all.

PLAIN CLOTHES MAN. I saw her accost you. I saw her try to detain you—and I've seen her do it before now.

MATT. I don't care what you've seen before now—you can't arrest her for that. You didn't see it this time.

PLAIN CLOTHES MAN. [*Still holding the* GIRL *and looking at* MATT *steadily*] You know perfectly well the woman accosted you—and you'd better keep out of this.

MATT. Let the girl go, then. You're exceeding your duty.

PLAIN CLOTHES MAN. What do you know about my duty? It's my duty to keep the park decent, man or woman. Now then, are you going to clear off?

MATT. No, I'm going to stay on.

PLAIN CLOTHES MAN. All right, then, you can follow us to the station.

MATT. Mayn't two people talk! I've made no complaint.

PLAIN CLOTHES MAN. I know this woman, I tell you. Don't interfere with me, or I shall want you too.

MATT. You can have me if you let the girl go.

PLAIN CLOTHES MAN. Now look here, I'm being very patient. But if you don't stop hindering me in the execution of my duty, I'll summon assistance and you'll *both* go to the station.

MATT. Don't lose your hair—I tell you, on my honour, this lady did not annoy me in the least. On the contrary——

PLAIN CLOTHES MAN. She was carrying on her profession here, as she's done before; my orders are to prevent that, and she's going to be charged. This is the third night I've watched her.

GIRL. I've never seen your face before.

PLAIN CLOTHES MAN. No, but I've seen yours—I've given you plenty of rope. That's enough, now——

> [*He puts his whistle in his mouth.*

MATT. It's a rotten shame! Drop that girl's arm!

> [*He lays his hand on the* PLAIN CLOTHES MAN's *arm.*
> *The* PLAIN CLOTHES MAN *blows his whistle, drops*
> *the* GIRL's *arm and seizes* MATT.

MATT. [*Breaking from him; to the* GIRL] Run for it!

GIRL. Oh! no—don't fight! The police have got it on you all the time. I'll go with him.

MATT. [*With fists up, keeping the* PLAIN CLOTHES MAN *at arm's-length*] Run, I tell you. He'll have his work cut out with me.

> [*But the* PLAIN CLOTHES MAN *is spryer than he thinks,*
> *runs in and catches him round the body.*

GIRL. Oh! Oh!

MATT. No, you don't!

> [*In the violent struggle the* PLAIN CLOTHES MAN's
> *bowler hat falls off.* MATT *emerges at arm's-length*
> *again, squaring up.*

MATT. Come on, then, if you will have it!

> [*The* PLAIN CLOTHES MAN *rushes in. He gets* MATT's
> *right straight from the shoulder on the point of the jaw,*
> *topples back, and goes down like a log.*

GIRL. Oh! Oh!

MATT. Run, you little idiot; run!

GIRL. [*Aghast*] Oh! he hit his head—on the rail! I heard the crack. See, he don't move!

MATT. Well, of course. I knocked him out. [*He goes a step nearer, looking down.*] The rail—did he——?

GIRL. [*Kneeling and feeling the* PLAIN CLOTHES MAN's *head*] Feel!

MATT. My God! That was a wump. I say!

GIRL. I told you not to fight. What did you want to fight for?

MATT. [*Pulling open the* PLAIN CLOTHES MAN'S *coat, and diving for his heart*] I can't feel it. Curse! Now we can't leave him. [*Feeling for the heart.*] Good God!

GIRL. [*Bending and snatching at his arm*] Quick! Before anybody comes. Across the grass back there. Who'd know?

MATT. [*Listening*] I can't leave the poor devil like this. [*Looking round.*] Take his hat; go and get some water in it from the Serpentine.

[*The* GIRL *picks up the hat and stands undecided.*

GIRL. [*Agonized*] No, no! Come away! It's awful, this! Suppose—suppose he's dead! [*She pulls at him.*

MATT. [*Shaking her off*] Don't be a little fool! Go and get some water. Go on!

[*The* GIRL *wrings her hands, then turns and runs off Left, with the hat.* MATT *continues to kneel, rubbing the* PLAIN CLOTHES MAN'S *temples, feeling his pulse, listening at his heart.*

MATT. I don't see how it's possible! [*With a gesture of despair he resumes his efforts to revive the body. Suddenly he looks up.*]

[*Two* POLICEMEN *have come from the Right.*

POLICEMAN. What's this?

MATT. I don't know. I'm a little afraid he——

POLICEMAN. What! Who is he? [*Looking at the face.*] Phew! One of ours! [*Bending, kneeling, putting the back of his hand to the mouth.*] Not a breath! How did this happen?

MATT. [*Pointing to the rail*] He knocked his head on that.

POLICEMAN. Where's his hat?

MATT. It fell off. Someone's gone to get water in it.

POLICEMAN. Who?

MATT. A girl——

POLICEMAN. He blew his whistle. Did you hit him?

MATT. There was a row. He seized me. I smote him on the jaw. He fell back and hit his head on the rail.

POLICEMAN. What was the row about?

MATT. [*Putting his hands to his head*] Oh! God knows! Original sin.

POLICEMAN. [*To the other* POLICEMAN] Mate, stay with him. I'll get an ambulance. [*To* MATT.] And you—come with me!

The curtain falls.

PART I

EPISODE I

More than a year has passed. On the prison farm, Dartmoor, in a heavy fog. The stone wall of the field runs along the back (on the back-cloth) and a stone wall joins it on the Left. MATT DENANT and a FELLOW CONVICT are picking up the potatoes they have dug up earlier. They are but dimly seen in the fog, flinging the potatoes right and left into two baskets between them. They are speaking in low voices.

MATT. The poor blighter was dead, and I got five years for manslaughter.

FELLOW CONVICT. Cripes! A cop! You were lucky not to swing, mate.

MATT. The girl stood by me like a brick. If she hadn't come forward——

FELLOW CONVICT. Lucky there, too. Most of 'em wouldn't. They're too mortal scared. 'Ow much you got left to do?

MATT. Three years, if I behave like a plaster saint.

[*He stops and straightens himself.*

FELLOW CONVICT. I got four. I say, you're a torf, yn't you?

MATT. Toff! [*With a laugh.*] Item, one Oxford accent; item, one objection to being spoken to like a dog.

FELLOW CONVICT. Hush! [*Jerking his thumb towards the wall, Right.*] Fog don't prevent 'em hearin', blight 'em!

MATT. It's come up mighty sudden. Think it's going to last?

FELLOW CONVICT. After a wet spell—this time o' year, when the wind's gone—yus. They'll be roundin' us up in a minute, you'll see—and 'ome to Blighty. Makes 'em nervous —fog. That's when you get the escapes.

MATT. No one's ever got away from here, they say.

FELLOW CONVICT. There've been a good few tries, though.

MATT. Gosh! I'd like to have one.

FELLOW CONVICT. Don't you do it, mate. You want clothes, you want money, you want a car, to give you a dawg's chance. And then they'd get you. This moor's the 'ell of a place. I say, you must 'ave hit that cop a fair knock!

MATT. Just an ordinary knock-out on the jaw. It wasn't that. He landed the back of his head on the Row rail. [*He resumes potato picking.*] Poor devil! He wasn't married, luckily.

FELLOW CONVICT. Luckily? Well, you never know about *that*. But get 'im off your chest, mate—'e wouldn't sit on mine—no more than an 'Un did in the War. That's a good fair potato. [*Holding one up.*

[*The figure of a* WARDER *is dimly seen coming along from the Right under the wall. He stops.*

WARDER. No talking there! When you've finished that row, pick back the next and then stand by to fall in. [*No answer from the* CONVICTS.] Hear me? Answer, can't you?

FELLOW CONVICT. Right, sir!

[*The* WARDER'S *figure is seen moving back.*
Nice man, ain't he? Wot'd I tell you? Early 'ome to tea.

MATT. [*Very low*] Like a dog! Three more years—like a dog!

FELLOW CONVICT. 'E's all right, reely. It's the fog. Fog makes 'em nervous; an' when a man's nervous I've always noticed 'e speaks like that.

MATT. Yes; well, *I* can't get used to it.

FELLOW CONVICT. Too particular, you torfs—get too much corn when you're two-year-olds.

MATT. [*Sharp and low*] *You* know the moor—where's Two Bridges?

FELLOW CONVICT. There—a mile.

MATT. And Tavistock?

FELLOW CONVICT. [*Pointing right back.*] Seven. Guv'nor—don't do it. There ain't a chance in a million. You'll only get pneumonium in this stinkin' wet, and they'll have you into the bargain, sure as eggs—bread and water, cells, and the rest of it.

MATT. I got out of Germany.

FELLOW CONVICT. Out of Germany! Cripes! That was none so dusty!

MATT. They've got no dogs here now, have they?

FELLOW CONVICT. Don't fancy they 'ave. But, Guv'nor, the whole countryside round 'ere's agynst you. They don't like convicts. Funny, yn't it?

[*They have reached the end of the row, Left, and stop, stooping, with their heads close together.*

MATT. Draw me a plan with this stick.

FELLOW CONVICT. Blimy! [*Marking the earth.*] 'Ere's the main road, and 'ere's the cross road to Tavistock. 'Ere's the Inn at Two Bridges, and 'ere's Post Bridge. 'Ere's Bee Tor Cross, ten to twelve mile. Chagford up there, Moreton 'Ampstead 'ere.

MATT. What's across the main road from Two Bridges?

FELLOW CONVICT. Moor. A long bit o' wood about 'ere; then 'Ambledon; then you drops into fields to Widecombe; then up, and more moor to Heytor and Bovey. [*Pronounce* BUVVY.] There's rail at Bovey or Lustleigh, or Moreton or Tavistock, and much good that'll do you with everybody as eager to see you as if you was the Prince of Wyles! Out this way you got Fox Tor Mire—ruddy bad bog, that!

[*A moment's silence while* MATT *studies the chart in the soil.*

WARDER'S VOICE. [*Off*] Hurry up with that last row—you two men! [*The fog grows thicker.*

MATT. [*Smearing out the chart with his foot*] It's real thick now. Gosh! I'll have a shot!

> [*They move back, Right, beginning the last row.*

FELLOW CONVICT. [*Jerking his thumb Left.*] There's another blighter thirty yards out on the wall there. 'E'll shoot.

MATT. I know. I'm going over that wall in the corner, and then along under his nose on the near side. Ten to one he'll be looking out on the off side in this fog. If that chap there [*Jerking his head Right*] doesn't spot me I'll get by.

FELLOW CONVICT. You're mad, Guv'nor. They'll shoot at sight. And if they don' see you—in ten minutes I'll have finished this row, an' they're bound to know you're gone. You 'aven't the chance of a cock-louse.

MATT. All right, friend, don't worry! A bullet'd be a nice change for me. If I don't get one—I'll give 'em a run for their money.

FELLOW CONVICT. Well, if you must go, mate—Strike the main road and run that way. [*Pointing.*] In this fog they'll 'ave to take us back before they dare start after you. You'll find a scrap of a wood a bit beyond the river on the left side. Get into it and cover yourself with leaves till it's dead dark. Then you'll still be close to the road and you can myke shift in a stack or something till the morning. If you go wandering about the moor all night in this fog, you won't get nowhere, and you'll be done in stiff before dawn.

MATT. Thanks. Sooner the better, now—Never stop to look at a fence. Next time the steam's full on. [*Puts some potatoes in his pocket.*] *Pommes crus—sauce Dartmoor*. Can one eat these raw? I ate turnips in Germany.

FELLOW CONVICT. Never tried, Guv'nor. Tyke this.

> [*He holds out a slice of bread.*

MATT. Thanks awfully. You're a good chap.

FELLOW CONVICT. Wish you luck. Wish I was comin' too, but I 'aven't got the pluck, an' that's a fact.

MATT. Now! Turn your head the other way and keep it there. Remember me to Blighty. So long!

> [*He moves three steps away from his fellow convict, pauses a few seconds, then suddenly, stooping low, runs to the wall, Left, and is over it like a cat. In the minute of silence that follows one can see the* CONVICT *listening.*

FELLOW CONVICT. [*Counting the seconds to himself, up to twenty, in an excited murmur*] Gawd! 'E's past that blighter! [*Listens again.*] Gawd! 'E's orf! [*With realization of his fellow's escape comes an itch to attempt it himself.*] Shall I 'ave a shoot meself? Shall I? Gawd! I must!

> [*He has just turned to sneak off, when the* WARDER's *voice is heard off, Right.*

WARDER. You, man, there! Where's your mate?

FELLOW CONVICT. 'Ad a call, sir.   [*He stands still.*

VOICE OF WARDER. [*Nearing*] What d'you mean?

FELLOW CONVICT. Went over to that wall, sir.

WARDER. [*Appearing*] He's not there. Now then! Where is he?

FELLOW CONVICT. No use arstin' me. *I* don' know where he is.

WARDER. Come with me. [*He marches sharply along the wall back towards the Left. Halting.*] Convict! Out there! Answer! Warder! You, Williams! Anyone passed you? Lost a man here!

VOICE OF SECOND WARDER. No one's passed.

FIRST WARDER. Sharp, then! There's a man gone!

> [SECOND WARDER *appears on the top of the wall.*

SECOND WARDER. He must ha' got past *you*, then.

FIRST WARDER. Curse this fog! Fire a shot for warning. No, don't, or we'll have others running for it. Muster sharp and get off home and report—that's the only thing. [*To* CONVICT.] Here, you! Keep your mouth shut. You know all about it, I bet.

FELLOW CONVICT. Not me, sir. 'E just said 'e 'ad a call to 'ave tea with the Duchess; an' I went on pickin' up, knowin' you was in an 'urry.

FIRST WARDER. Mind your lip! Come on, Williams. March, you!

They are marching, Right, as the curtain falls.

EPISODE II

Seven hours have passed. The moor in the dark and the fog, close to the main road. Nothing visible.

VOICE OF FIRST WARDER. What the hell's the use of picketing this blighted road—you can see nothing!

VOICE OF SECOND WARDER. I've seen two cops made just here. When a man's out on a night like this, it's human nature to cling to the road.

FIRST WARDER. But he may be anywhere.

SECOND WARDER. If he's travelling at all, he's on a road. You can't make it on the moor in fog as thick as this.

FIRST WARDER. He may have headed for Cornworthy.

SECOND WARDER. They never go that way—too afraid of Fox Tor Mire.

FIRST WARDER. Or Tavistock?

SECOND WARDER. Well, that road's picketed all right.

FIRST WARDER. I'd flog for escapes. They never think of us—out after these blighters nights like this. It's too bad, you know. Got a drain of the stuff?

SECOND WARDER. Here you are. Put it to your mouth by the smell.

FIRST WARDER. If I get this cove, I'll let him know it. 'Tisn't in nature not to feel murderous towards a chap that keeps you out all night in this sort o' muck! [*He drinks.*

SECOND WARDER. Leave some for me, mate. [*In a whisper.*] What was that? Hark! [*They listen.*

FIRST WARDER. Don't 'ear nothing.

        [*He is about to put the flask to his mouth again.*

SECOND WARDER. Thought I heard a scraping noise. Shall I show a glim?

FIRST WARDER. Better not!   [*They listen.*

SECOND WARDER. There's ponies round here.

FIRST WARDER. This fellow was a toff.

SECOND WARDER. Um! Captain in the War.

FIRST WARDER. Him that killed the 'tec in Hyde Park. He's a sporty beggar. Got blood in him. That's the worst sort when it comes to an escape—they run till they drop.

SECOND WARDER. Man of education—might have had more sense than to run for it. He must know he can't get off.

FIRST WARDER. There's a spirit in some of these higher-class chaps you can't break. D'you know that lawyer in the left wing—embezzlement? That chap gives me the creeps. He's got the self-possession of an image.

SECOND WARDER. I'm sorry for some of these fellows, but I'm damned if I'm ever sorry for a gentleman. They ought to know better than to get themselves here. And, as you say, they've got the devil's brass.

FIRST WARDER. Still—up on the ladder and down with a whump—it hits 'em harder than it does the others.

SECOND WARDER. [*Yawning*] Wish I was in bed! [*Startingly.*] There it is again! [*They listen.*] It'll be a pony. A warder's life's about the limit. If it wasn't for the missus, I'd sooner sweep streets.

FIRST WARDER. I've got used to it, barring a circus like this. The devil himself couldn't get used to that. It's only fit for the movies.

SECOND WARDER. I believe you. Did you see that picture with Duggie in it? 'Ow'd you think 'e does that roof business? We got some pretty tidy cat burglars, but I don't believe there's one could do what he does.

FIRST WARDER. Well, I'll tell you. I think he has spring heels; and I notice his hands are very blurry in the picture. I believe he holds a rope, and they take that out afterwards, by some process.

SECOND WARDER. Never thought o' that! But when he falls and catches on that ledge?

FIRST WARDER. That's an optical deception. Some of those movie jossers ought to be in prison, the way they deceive the public.

SECOND WARDER. I never saw anything on the screen I liked better than "My Old Dutch"! That fair got me. I took the missus, and I tell you there wasn't a dry eye about the pair of us.

FIRST WARDER. Charlie knocks *me*. I feel a better man after I've seen 'im. Now, why is that?

SECOND WARDER. 'E's very 'uman. Must make a pot of money.

FIRST WARDER. I'm wet through—give me another drain. [*Gurgling sounds.*] If I catch that chap, you'll 'ave to stop me quick, or I'll manhandle him for sure.

SECOND WARDER. Same here. We'd better toss up which stops the other. Call!

FIRST WARDER. 'Eads.

SECOND WARDER. Which is it? Throw a glim.

    [*The* FIRST WARDER *throws from an electric torch the first light of the scene. Their two faces, on the footlight side of the road, are seen close together over the coin.*

SECOND WARDER. Tails—You've lost. [*The glim is dowsed.*] 'Ow do we stand, then? Do I stop you, or do you stop me?

FIRST WARDER. You stop me.

SECOND WARDER. No, I won. That means *I* get the go at him. Lawd Gawd! what a night! Just feel if that rope's all right across the road.

FIRST WARDER. It's taut. Bit too low, though—ought to catch him mid-thigh by rights.

SECOND WARDER. You trust me, old hoss; if it catches 'im as high as that, he stops and goes off sideways, or turns and runs back. It should catch him just below the knee. Then, ten to one he goes over, and we're on to him before he can get up. He'll be goin' a good bat, remember. You'll find me on 'is 'ead when you come to stoppin' me.

FIRST WARDER. To think we can't even smoke. D'you hold with givin' prisoners tobacco, Williams?

SECOND WARDER. On the whole, I do. It sweetens 'em, and that's better for us. I'd give 'em two pipes a week, and stop 'em if they gave a warder any trouble. I've got one or two fellers I'm quite fond of. I'd be glad for 'em to have a smoke every day. Listen! [*They listen. In a whisper.*] Footsteps! They are!

FIRST WARDER. Yes.

SECOND WARDER. [*Still in a whisper*] Look here, mate! Just before he gets to the rope, I'll throw the light into his face, then dowse it sharp. He'll start to run forward and go head foremost. Stand by!   [*They listen.*

FIRST WARDER. He's comin' on! Suppose it isn't him?

SECOND WARDER. Must chance that. I'll throw the light as I say——

> [*A moment of utter black tenseness, during which the foot-*
> *steps are heard clearer and clearer.*]

Now! Stand by!

> [*He flashes the light on the figure of* MATT *advancing along*
> *the road.   The light is dowsed, the* WARDERS *rush forward.*
> *Darkness and the sound of a scramble.*

SECOND WARDER'S VOICE. I've got him!

FIRST WARDER'S VOICE. [*Half strangled*] No, you ruddy fool—you've got me!

> *The curtain falls.*

EPISODE III

*Thirty-two hours have passed.   A bedroom at an Inn on the moor.
Dark with streaks of daylight coming in from two curtained
windows, back, opening on to a long balcony.   Between them
a bed juts into the room.   Right, forward, a dressing-table
with chair.   Left, back, a washstand.   Left, forward, a door
opening inwards.   At foot of the bed a chair with a woman's
undergarments thrown on it.   A dressing-gown over the foot-
rail of the bed, some slippers on the left side of the bed.   A
SHINGLED LADY asleep in the bed.   Knocking on the door,
Left.*

LADY. [*Sleepily*] Come in!
    [*A MAID enters with a can of hot water, which she places
        on the washstand, Left.*
MAID. 'Alf past seven, madam.
LADY. [*Yawning*] What sort of day?
MAID. Foggy still.   Taking a bath, madam?
LADY. Yes.   Oh!   My husband's coming back this
evening.   I'm to be moved back to the double room.
MAID. Yes, madam; they told me.
    [*She has drawn aside the curtains, Left, and now moves
        round and draws back the curtains, Right.*]
That escaped convict, madam; they haven't got him yet.
LADY. No?   How thrilling!
MAID. It's the fog.   He's been out nearly two days.   They
say it's the young man who killed the detective in Hyde Park,
that made such a fuss.
LADY. Oh?   That Captain Denant!   I remember.   It
might have been worse, then.
MAID. Of course they'll catch him—no one ever gets off.
LADY. Don't they?
MAID. Oh!   no, madam!   It wouldn't never do.

LADY. I should have thought in fog like this——

MAID. You see, they got to eat and get clothes. That's where they're caught.

LADY. [*Yawning*] This horrible fog!—one can't ride or fish, or even walk.   Shall I get up, or shall I——?

MAID. [*Rather coldly*] Just as you please, madam.

LADY. [*With a laugh*] Well, I suppose I'd better.

MAID. I'll turn the bath on.

LADY. Thank you.

> [*The* MAID *goes out, and the* LADY, *in her pyjamas, emerges from bed, feels for her slippers, and puts on her dressing-gown.   She goes to a window, and looks out. It is a French window, and slightly open on a short hook.*

LADY. Ugh!   What a day!

> [*Taking sponge and bath towel from the washstand she goes to the door and out.   As soon as the door is shut there is a commotion where the bed touches the wall, and from behind the window curtain* MATT DENANT *cautiously emerges, glances quickly round, and stretches himself.   He looks haggard, sodden, and crumpled, and has his boots in his hand.*

MATT. [*Muttering*] A lady!   Dash it!   I must get out!

> [*He goes to the window and looks cautiously out, then recoils, drawing in his breath with a hiss.   Then, after once more glancing round the room, he steps to the door.*

LADY'S VOICE. [*Off*] I simply can't take cold baths!

> [MATT *flattens himself against the wall, so that he will be behind the door if it is opened.   And suddenly it is.*

LADY'S VOICE. [*In doorway*] Let me know when the water's hot, please.

MAID'S VOICE. [*Off*] Yes, madam.

> *The* LADY *re-enters, and passing the door knob from her right hand to her left behind her as she naturally would,*

closes it without seeing MATT, *and crosses to the*
dressing-table, where she sits down and takes up a
brush to brush her shingled hair. MATT *moves*
quickly to the door, and has his hand on the handle,
when his image passes into the mirror. The LADY
drops the brush, and faces round with an exclamation on
her open mouth.

MATT. Hush! It's quite O.K.

LADY. Who—how—what d'you mean by coming into my
room?

[MATT *drops the door handle, turning the key in the lock.*

MATT. [*In a low voice*] Really, I'm most frightfully sorry.

[*Suddenly the fact that he is the escaped convict dawns on her.*

LADY. You're the escaped—— [*She starts up to go to the*
window and call for help ; but stops at the gestures he makes.]

MATT. I wonder if you'd mind awfully speaking pianissimo.

LADY. [*Tensely*] What made you come in here? How did
you get in?

MATT. I've been under the bed for hours. You see, I
couldn't tell it was a lady.

LADY. D'you mean my hair?

MATT. Oh no! I couldn't see that.

LADY. I didn't snore?

MATT. No; but that's not an infallible test of sex. I
didn't either, or you'd have heard me.

LADY. D'you mean to say you went to sleep?

MATT. I'm afraid I did. Of course, if I'd known——

[*A pause.*

LADY. Well, as you're a gentleman, aren't you going?

MATT. I'd simply love to. But where?

LADY. Really, I can't tell you.

MATT. Look at me! What can one do in these togs?

LADY. D'you expect me to lend you some?

MATT. Hardly. But I'd be eternally grateful if you'd give
me something to eat.

LADY. [*Opening a drawer and taking out some chocolate*] This is pretty cool, you know. I ought to ring and hand you over.

MATT. Yes. But—you look such a sport.

LADY. [*Subtly flattered*] I know who you are. Your name's in the paper. But do you realize my position?

MATT. Afraid I only realize my own.

LADY. If I don't hand you over, how on earth are you going to get out of here without being seen?

MATT. Might I have that chocolate?

LADY. [*Taking it from the dressing-table drawer*] It's only local.

MATT. That won't deter me. I've been forty hours on a piece of bread and two raw potatoes. [*He takes the chocolate, bites some off, and puts the rest in his pocket.*] Would you mind frightfully if I drank some water?

LADY. Of course not.

> [MATT *goes over to the washstand. When his back is turned she springs to action, but instead of going to door or window, rapidly conceals underneath the bedclothes the corsets and underclothes flung on the chair at the foot of the bed, then returns to the dressing-table.* MATT *is drinking deeply.*

MATT. [*Turning*] That's good. Ever had the hunted feeling? [*She shakes her head.*] Well, don't! A coursed hare is nothing to it. Oh! I am so jolly stiff!

LADY. [*Thrilled in spite of herself*] Do you know you're only three miles from the Prison?

MATT. I do. The first night I meant to get near Exeter by morning, and where d'you think I was? A mile from where I started. I'd been ringing. That's what you do in fog. Is that a razor?

LADY. [*On stilts*] My husband's. Why? [*As* MATT *takes it up.*] No! There's a limit, Captain Denant. You can't have a weapon.

MATT. No, of course! But would you mind awfully if I shaved? You see, like this [*Passes his hand over his chin*] I haven't an earthly, even if I could get clothes. There's nothing more attractive than a three days' beard. [*While speaking he has lathered himself without a brush.*] I'm a very quick shaver. It takes me three minutes. I can do it in thirty-two and a half strokes.

LADY. [*Gasping*] Well, I never—It takes me [*hand to her neck*]—that is—I mean—Have you nearly been caught?

MATT. [*Between scraping motions of the razor*] Twice I've been within twenty feet of the hounds——

LADY. Hounds!

MATT. Human! Just out of their jaws. [*Groans.*] D'you know anything so frightful as a shave like this?

LADY. Well, really——

MATT. I mean except, of course, not having it.

LADY. How did you get in here?

MATT. You see, I *did* so want a dry night, so I hid up and waited till every light was out. I tried to get in below, and couldn't; then I made a boss shot at the corner of the balcony and fell on my back—— Did you feel a sort of earthquake? No? I did. When I got over that, I had another shot at a pillar and made it that time. I chose your window because it was open—hooked it up again and slid straight under the bed. I meant to sneak some clothes, and be off before daylight, but I only woke up when the maid came in. [*She indicates a towel; he steeps it in water and wipes his face.*] D'you mind if I put on my boots? [*He stoops and puts them on.*

LADY. So you actually slept under there?

MATT. Alas! I did.

LADY. Well! It's about the limit.

MATT. Will be if I get clear—no one ever has.

LADY. Tell me, Captain Denant, weren't you at Harcheston with my brother—he used to talk of a Matt Denant, who was an awfully good runner.

MATT. Quite likely.   I was at school with an awful lot of brothers.   What was his name?

LADY. No.   That won't do.

MATT. You're right.   Never tell a convict anything he can tell anybody else.

LADY. I really don't see how I can help you.

MATT. Nor do I, worse luck!

LADY. I read your trial.

MATT. [*Standing up*] And you think me a bad lot, of course. [*Bitterly*.] D'you know how I spend most of my time in prison? Holding imaginary conversations with the respectable.

LADY. [*With a smile*] Respectable!   D'you think you're holding a real one now?

MATT. I certainly don't. . . . I . . . I beg your pardon. . . . You know what I mean.   But I bet most people have put me down a rotter.

LADY. Was all you said true?

MATT. Gospel.

LADY. I suppose they do hunt those girls rather.

MATT. Yes, but you know, I didn't even really see red. I've been sorry enough for that poor chap.

LADY. Well, Captain Denant, what now?

MATT. You've been most awfully kind and I don't want to impose on you; but I shall never get out of here as I am.

LADY.   Why not?

MATT. [*Jerking his head towards the window*] They're too thoughtful.   There's a picket out there.

> [*The* LADY *turns to the window and looks out ; then she turns to* MATT *and finds him smiling.*]

Oh! No, I wasn't scared.   One doesn't give one's own kind away.

LADY. I don't know that.   Go and try some of those other rooms.   Try the couple next door to me.

> [*A knock on the door.* BOTH *stand alert.*

LADY. Yes?

Voice of Maid. [*Off*] The bath water's hot now, madam.

Lady. All right. Thank you. [*Her finger is on her lips.*] D'you think she could hear us?

Matt. Hope not. [*Going close.*] Thanks most awfully. You don't know how decent it's been after a year in there, to talk to a lady. I won't leave any traces.

Lady. What are you going to do?

Matt. Wait till he's looking the other way, sneak along the balcony, drop at the end, and bolt for it again.

Lady. Are you still a good runner?

Matt. Pretty fair, if I wasn't so stiff.

Lady. [*After a long look at him*] No! Look here! When I go to my bath I'll make sure there's no one. If I don't come back, slip down the stairs, they're almost opposite. In the hall, hanging, you'll find my husband's old Burberry and fishing basket, rod, and fishing hat; a long brown Burberry, with stains, and flies in the hat. Put them on and go out of the front door; the river's down to the left. Can you fish? [*At his nod.*] You'd better, then. The bathroom's not that side, so I shan't see you. But—whistle "Lady, be good," if you know it.

Matt. Rather! It's the only tune that's got into prison. Well, I can't thank you—you're just a brick!

[*He holds out his hand.*

Lady. [*Taking it*] Good luck! [*She passes him to the door.*] Wait a second! [*Getting a flask from drawer.*] Take this. If you see anyone looking at you—drink! Nothing gives one more confidence in a man than to see him drinking.

Matt. Splendid! What are you going to say to your husband?

Lady. Um! Yes! He comes to-night. Well, if he doesn't like it, he'll have to lump it. Oh! And these two pounds. It's all I've got here.

[*She has taken two pounds out of her bag lying on the dressing-table.*

B

MATT. [*Moved*] By George! I think you're sublime!

LADY. I'm afraid I doubt it.

MATT. If I'm caught, I shall say I pinched everything, of course; and if I get clear, I'll——

LADY. Oh! don't bother about that! Get behind the door now.

> [MATT *gets behind the door, and she opens it and goes out. After a moment she returns.*

LADY. All clear!

> [*Then, closing the door behind her, she goes.* MATT *takes a look round the room to see that he has not left any trace, and moves softly to the door. His hand is on the handle, when it is opened by the* MAID; *he has just time to shrink behind it while she stands looking curiously round the room, as if for somebody or something.*

LADY'S VOICE. [*Off*] Ellen! D'you mind going and getting me the suit I sent down to dry last night?

MAID. [*Starting*] Yes, madam. [*She goes, closing the door.*

> [MATT *has just time for a breath of relief when it is opened again and the* LADY *reappears.*

LADY. [*Seeing him breathless*] This is a bit hectic. [*In a whisper.*] Now! Quick!

> [MATT *dives past her. She stands a moment, hustles out her underclothing from under the bedclothes, then drawing the door to, goes to the window, opens it a little wider, and stands there listening. In half a minute the faint strains of " Lady, be good," whistled, are heard.*

LADY. [*Waving a stocking like a hat. Under her breath.*] Gone away!

> [*Whistling, " Lady, be good," she crosses jauntily towards the door, meeting the* MAID, *who is coming in with the dried suit. Continuing to whistle, she passes her with a roll of the eyes, leaving the* MAID *in three minds as The curtain falls.*

PART II

EPISODE IV

*Seven hours have passed.   Dartmeet.   An open space of fern and
grass above the river and away from trippers.*

> [MATT, *who has been working along the river all the
> morning, is squatting with his catch beside him—some
> eight smallish trout.   He is eating the last of his
> chocolate and drinking diligently from the already
> empty flask.   The more so as an* OLD GENTLEMAN
> *in Lovat tweeds is straying towards him.* MATT
> *begins taking his rod to pieces.*

OLD GENTLEMAN. [*Approaching from Left*] Afternoon!
Cleared up too well for *you*, I'm afraid.

MATT. Yes, it's a bit bright now.

OLD GENTLEMAN. Best eating in the world, those little
brown chaps.   Except perhaps the blue trout in the Tirol.
" Blaue forellen " with butter and potatoes, and a bottle of
Vöslauer Goldeck, eh?

MATT. My Golly, yes !   [*He looks wolfishly at his trout.*

OLD GENTLEMAN. [*Eyeing him askance*] Very foggy this
morning.   Worst point about the moor, these fogs.   Only
good for convicts—um?

MATT. [*Subduing a start*] Escapes, you mean?   But they
never get clear, I believe.

OLD GENTLEMAN. No, I'm told; but they try, you know—
they try.   I've often wondered what I should do if I blundered
into an escaped convict.

MATT. Yes, sir; bit of a problem.

OLD GENTLEMAN. [*Sitting down on his overcoat*] Between the Law and one's gentlemanly instincts—if it's gentlemanlike to dally with a felon—I wonder!

MATT. [*Warming to the subject*] A chap who tries to escape must be a sportsman, anyway. He takes a pretty long chance.

OLD GENTLEMAN. Yes, I don't envy a man in this country; we're a law-abiding people. I remember being very much struck with the difference in America last year—vital race, that—sublime disregard of the law themselves, and a strong sense of moral turpitude in others. Been in America?

MATT. I was out West ranching when the war broke out.

OLD GENTLEMAN. Indeed! Judging by the films, escaping justice is still fashionable there. I think I prefer a more settled country.

MATT. Personally, I've got rather a complex. Escaped from Germany in the war.

OLD GENTLEMAN. Did you? How very interesting!

MATT. If you want to get thin. It's a top-hole cure for adipose. An escape's no picnic.

OLD GENTLEMAN. I imagine not, indeed. Where did you get over the border?

MATT. Holland, after three days and nights on beets and turnips. Do you know the turnip in a state of nature, sir? He's a homely fellow—only beaten by the beet. Beg your pardon, sir, it slipped out. By the way, a convict got off the day before yesterday.

OLD GENTLEMAN. Yes, I saw that—a Captain Matt Denant. I read his case with interest at the time. How did it strike you?

MATT. [*On guard*] Don't believe I remember it.

OLD GENTLEMAN. What? The Hyde Park case?

MATT. Oh! Ah! yes. There was a girl. In those cases they might wait till you complain.

OLD GENTLEMAN. The detective was undoubtedly doing his

duty. And yet, quite a question—Rather dangerous giving the police a discretion on morals. The police are very like ourselves; and—er—most of us haven't got discretion, and the rest haven't got morals. The young man didn't complain, I think. D'you happen to recollect?

MATT. [*With an uneasy look*] So far as I remember, he said she was an intellectual.

[*The* OLD GENTLEMAN *has taken out a cigar-case and is offering it.*

OLD GENTLEMAN. Smoke?

MATT. Thanks very much. I've got into a bad habit of coming out without tobacco.   [*They bite and light cigars.*

OLD GENTLEMAN. I suppose one might run across that convict fellow any moment. It would be a little like meeting an adder. The poor thing only wants to get away from you. And yet, if you don't break its back, ten to one it'll bite a dog. I had two dogs die of snakebite. It's a duty, perhaps—what do you say?

MATT. Probably. But I don't always do mine.

OLD GENTLEMAN. Oh! don't you? I'm so glad of that. Neither do I.

MATT. Do you know that prison? It's a bad style of architecture.

OLD GENTLEMAN. No. The fact is, I've had the misfortune in my time to send a good many people to prison. And in those days I did make a point of seeing a prison now and then. I remember I used to give my Juries a pass to go and see where they sent their fellow-beings. Once I tested whether they went to look round or not, and out of three Juries—no, it was four—how many do you think had had the curiosity?

MATT. None.

OLD GENTLEMAN. Isn't that a little cynical? [*With his sideway, bird-like glance.*] No, it was—one. Ha!

MATT. Who'd want to go into a prison? I'd as soon visit the Morgue. The bodies there aren't *living*, anyway.

OLD GENTLEMAN. They tell me prisons are much improved. They've introduced a human feeling.

MATT. Have they? Splendid! What was the date of that?

OLD GENTLEMAN. [*His eyes busy*] They've abolished the arrows, anyway. And I believe they don't shave their heads now. Do you know any convicts?

MATT. [*With a wriggle*] I? No. Only one.

OLD GENTLEMAN. Indeed? And is he interesting?

MATT. The most interesting chap I know.

OLD GENTLEMAN. Ha! Suppose this escaped convict suddenly turned up here. [*Jerking his thumb towards* MATT.] What should you do?

MATT. Run like a hare.

OLD GENTLEMAN. Dear me, yes. I think it would depend on whether anyone was about. Human nature is very—er—sensitive. D'you find this climate bracing? Dartmoor has quite a reputation.

MATT. Overrated—I think.

OLD GENTLEMAN. You know it well?

MATT. No; this is my first visit.

OLD GENTLEMAN. And will you be here long?

MATT. Hope not.

OLD GENTLEMAN. Beautiful spot—Dartmeet!

MATT. I prefer Two Bridges.

[*Putting up his rod and whistling " Lady, be good."*

OLD GENTLEMAN. Ah! What fly have you been using?

MATT. Just a tag.

OLD GENTLEMAN. I've not fished for years. [*As* MATT *suddenly passes his hand over his brow under his hat.*] Anything the matter?

MATT. Afraid I shall have to abandon your excellent cigar. I've enjoyed it, but I'm smoking on a rather empty stomach.

[*He looks ruefully at the unsmoked portion of his cigar, and pitches it away.*

OLD GENTLEMAN. Dear me! Yes. I remember that feeling coming over me once at the Royal Academy banquet—just before I had to make a speech. [*Another of his bird-like glances.*] Tobacco must be one of the great deprivations in prison, I always think. Didn't you find that so in—in—Germany?

MATT. [*Breathing rather fast and completing the dismantlement of his fishing rod*] Oh! we got tobacco now and then.

OLD GENTLEMAN. And empty stomachs too, I'm afraid.

MATT. Yes.

OLD GENTLEMAN. One never ceases to be grateful to those who endured such things. [*Offering his cigar case.*] Will you try again after tea? These moor teas with cream and jam.

MATT. [*Taking it*] Well, thank you, sir. I shall down him next time.

> [MATT *is now ready for departure, for he has been getting increasingly uneasy with this* OLD GENTLEMAN. *He takes up his basket and lays the fish within it.*

OLD GENTLEMAN. Well [*Getting up*] I must be getting on too. It's been very pleasant. I've enjoyed our little talk. At my time of life one doesn't often get new sensations.

MATT. [*Nonplussed*] Good Lord, sir! Have I given you any?

OLD GENTLEMAN. Well, I don't remember ever having talked before to a prisoner who'd escaped from—Germany.

MATT. Good-bye, sir.

OLD GENTLEMAN. Good-bye, Captain Denant—[MATT *starts.*] I hope you'll have a pleasant journey, especially as no one seems to have noticed our little chat.

MATT. [*Staring at him*] D'you mind frightfully telling me how you spotted me?

OLD GENTLEMAN. Not at all! First, the way you looked at your trout—shall I say—er—wolfishly? And then—forgive me—your legs.

MATT. [*Drawing up his Burberry and contemplating his legs*] Yes. I hoped you'd think I was a leader of fashion.

OLD GENTLEMAN. And there was another thing—your obvious sympathy with yourself.

MATT. That's a prison habit, sir. You're not allowed to sympathize with other people, for fear of contaminating them. Before I got into quod I don't remember ever feeling sorry for myself. But I doubt if I shall ever again feel sorry for anyone else.

OLD GENTLEMAN. That must be very natural. Well, it's been most interesting, because now you see I know what I should do——

MATT. [*Intently*] Is it indiscreet to ask, sir?

OLD GENTLEMAN. Well, Captain Denant, this time—I say *this* time—wink the other eye. Good-day to you!

MATT. Good-day, sir. It's most frightfully sporting of you. For the moment I feel quite human.

OLD GENTLEMAN. Do you know, that's been rather the effect on me. Original sin, I suppose. Good-day!

[*He goes off, watching the smoke of his cigar and smiling
faintly to himself. On* MATT, *affected by kindness,
The curtain falls.*

EPISODE V

An hour has passed. On the Moor; a high spot.

[FOUR TRIPPERS, *two men and two women, disgorged from a
Ford car, are picnicking. One of the men, about fifty,
in blue clothes, has a Merchant Service look and a
concertina; the other looks more like a shopkeeper,
and is perhaps fifty-five. His wife is a stout woman,
about forty, of mellow appearance. The other
woman is the shopkeeper's sister, dried-up and
spinsterish. Their clothes are of a suitable nature—
some feathers. They are all eating heavily.*

WIFE. Captain, you're a prophet—considerin' what it was when we left Ashburton. I call this lovely! [*Eats.*

CAPTAIN. Takes a bit o' weather to flummox a sailor, ma'am. [*Drinks.*

WIFE. "You trust the Captain," I said to Pinkem this morning, didn't I, father? *I* knew, you see; [*archly*] my corns weren't shootin'.

SISTER. That's not very nice, Fanny.

WIFE. Why not? I'd like to see someone who 'asn't corns, if the truth was known. 'Ave another of these cut rounds, Dolly, and cheer up. Father, don't you eat any more cream—your eyes are yeller.

SHOPKEEPER. When I first came to Devonshire I could put away 'alf a pound o' cream at a meal.

WIFE. Yes, and it spoiled your temper for life.

SHOPKEEPER. Am I bad-tempered, Dolly?

SISTER. So-so, James.

SHOPKEEPER. What do you say, Captain?

CAPTAIN. You keep it for your wife, my boy. Outside the bosom of your family you're a perfect cherub.

WIFE. Captain, you're an 'opeless Benedick.

CAPTAIN. Bachelor born, ma'am.

WIFE. With a wife in every port, eh?

SISTER. Oh! That reely isn't nice, Fanny; so old-fashioned too.

CAPTAIN. Is it, ma'am?

WIFE. Now, Captain, don't go shockin' Dolly. Oh! There's an insect on my skirt! I never seen one like it.

SHOPKEEPER. Kill it, then.

WIFE. Why?

SHOPKEEPER. Always kill what you don't know.

WIFE. [*Flipping it off*] It's only a biddle—poor thing! Give us a tune, Captain.

[*The* CAPTAIN *draws a long blast from his concertina.*
Hallo! 'Oo's this?

[MATT, *in Burberry, with rod and basket, has appeared*
        Left, and stands lifting his hat.

MATT. Afternoon! Wonder if you could put me right for
Bovey?

SHOPKEEPER. Bovey! That's a goodish step—matter of
twelve miles, I should say.

MATT. My Lord! Not really?

SHOPKEEPER. You go down the 'ill, through Ponsworthy to
Widecombe, and up the 'ill, turn to the left, and ask again.

MATT. I see. Will there be anyone to ask?

SHOPKEEPER. I shouldn't think so.

CAPTAIN. Had any sport, sir?

MATT. [*Opening the basket*] Eight, rather small.

WIFE. My! Don't they look nice! Such good eatin',
too.

MATT. Would you like them, ma'am?

WIFE. [*With affected restraint*] I'm sure it's very good of you.

CAPTAIN. Don't you miss the chance, Mrs. Pinkem;
nothing like moor trout, with a moor appetite.

SISTER. [*Distantly*] I'm *sure* it's most kind, from a stranger.

WIFE. [*Suddenly*] Well, I don't know, if you're so obliging.
'And me the *Daily Mail*, father. I'll wrap 'em up; and thank
you very much. I quite appreciate it.

MATT. That's splendid! [*He hands them.*] Turned out quite
nice, hasn't it? Have you come far?

SHOPKEEPER. From Ashburton—ten mile.

MATT. Heard anything there of the escaped convict?

SHOPKEEPER. What about it? Haven't looked at the paper
last day or two.

WIFE. Another escape!—Oh, my!

MATT. Rather! He got off in the fog, night before last.

SISTER. I always hate to think of one of those dreadful men
at large. You can't sleep in your bed.

CAPTAIN. Don't you get *too* excited, ma'am. Think of the
choice 'e's got.

WIFE. [*Scanning the paper*] Why! It's the man that killed the poor detective in 'Yde Park! That villain! It says 'ere they nearly got him—twice.

[MATT, *who is eyeing them closely, eyes a loaf even more closely, and tries to manœuvre into a position to annex it.*

SHOPKEEPER. I 'ope everybody's helping to catch him. He must be a regular desperado. That was a bad case. I never believed the girl.

SISTER. I should think not, indeed!

SHOPKEEPER. Nor the young man neither. They were up to no good there. They tell me those London parks are in a proper state.

CAPTAIN. They ain't a Sunday School, that's certain.

WIFE. Fie, Captain!

SISTER. [*Acidly*] I believe some people quite sympathized with him. Fancy!

MATT. Well, if you won't think it too eccentric, I did, for one.

SHOPKEEPER. You!—Why?

MATT. I thought he had devilish hard luck.

SHOPKEEPER. Ah! there's always a fuss made about the Law. You can't even 'ang a woman for murderin' her 'usband without a lot o' 'ysterical nonsense. Look at that case not long ago—there was a petition as long as your arm.

CAPTAIN. I remember. The young chap was a steward. I don't recall this Hyde Park case.

WIFE. Why! the detective arrested one o' those women this young man had been sittin' with—a gentleman he was too—and if he didn't 'it him an' break 'is 'ead, an' kill 'im, poor man!

CAPTAIN. Then why didn't they string him up?

MATT. The jury found it was a quarrel, not an attempt to evade arrest. Besides, in falling the detective hit his head on the iron railing of the Row, and the doctors said he died of the concussion.

SHOPKEEPER. That didn't ought to have got 'im off.
He hit the man. If 'e 'adn't 'it him, 'e wouldn't have
fallen.

MATT. Exactly! Brilliant! But if the detective hadn't
seized him, he wouldn't have hit him.

SHOPKEEPER. Well! *I'd* 'ave hung 'im.

WIFE. Don't be so bloodthirsty, father!

SHOPKEEPER. Well, I would! Hitting an officer for doing
his duty. Sitting with a woman in the Park, too! He only
got off because he was quality.

MATT. Don't you think that's a superstition?

> [*The* SHOPKEEPER *glares at him, but decides that he is a
> gentleman, and therefore prejudiced, and only snorts
> slightly.*

SISTER. Did they punish the woman?

MATT. What for, ma'am?

SISTER. *I'd* keep them shut up; then they wouldn't tempt
young men—the 'arpies!

MATT. [*Unexpectedly*] Oh! God!

> [*They all stare at him.   Then the* SHOPKEEPER *fatuously
> breaks the silence.*

SHOPKEEPER. Can't say I was ever tempted by a woman.

MATT. No, you've got a Ford car, I see. D'you find them
good in this sort of country?

SHOPKEEPER. [*Distantly*] I do, sir.

MATT. Do they get up these hills?

SHOPKEEPER. I should think so. I'd engage to catch any
convict with my car.

MATT. Would you?   [*A thought strikes him.*]   Splendid!

WIFE. Well, I think we ought to be gettin' 'ome. 'And
me the teapot, Captain. Now, Dolly! Never mind those
bits o' cake and bread—they're no good. Just leave the
deebris. I'd like to be in before dark, with a convict loose
like this. He might come prowlin' round, pickin' things up.

> [MATT *with a secret movement pockets some scraps.*

MATT. Good afternoon! Hope you'll enjoy the trout.

[*He moves away out of the picture.*

WIFE and CAPTAIN. Good afternoon—Good afternoon, sir!

[MATT *salutes and vanishes, Right.*

SISTER. Here, Fanny! Did you see him pocket the scraps?

WIFE. No! Why, he's a gentleman—didn't you hear his sniffy way o' talkin'?

SISTER. I saw him with my own eyes—two bits of cake and a round.   [*Sound of a car being started.*

SHOPKEEPER. I say! [*Jumping up.*] What's 'e doin' with the Ford?

CAPTAIN. Hi, there! You, sir!

SHOPKEEPER. He's got in. Hi!

SISTER. The villain!

ALL. Hi! hi! hi!

[*Sounds of a levanting car, and a halloed "So long!"*
[*The TWO MEN run out of the picture.*

WIFE. Well, I——

SISTER. *You!* Taking his fish like that! You might ha' known he was a thief. Why—why—of course! He's the— oh! oh!

WIFE. Dry up, Dolly! 'Ow are we to get 'ome?

[*The TWO MEN run back into the picture, breathless.*

SHOPKEEPER. Well, of all the impudent villains!

CAPTAIN. I'm jiggered!

[*He sits down with his hands on his knees and goes off into wheezy laughter.*

SISTER. 'Ow *can* you? 'Ow *can* you, Captain? And we talking about him all the time!

CAPTAIN. [*Stopping*] What! Him!

SISTER. The escaped convict! He hadn't the leggins of a gentleman.

CAPTAIN. What! Did *you* look at his legs, ma'am?

WIFE. It's all your fault, Pinkem; you and Dolly's— callin' 'im names. If you 'adn't called 'im names, he wouldn't 'a stole the car—talkin' of hanging 'im! I could see 'im gettin' heated.

SHOPKEEPER. You called 'im a villain yourself. Well—Bovey—we know where to look for him.

CAPTAIN. A blind, old bean.

SHOPKEEPER. I say 'e will go there.

CAPTAIN. I say e' won't.

SHOPKEEPER. I say 'e'll see we'll think 'e won't, and put the double cross on us.

CAPTAIN. Well, I say, 'e'll see we'll think 'e's going to put the double cross on us.

WIFE. Oh! My corns!

SISTER. Impudence, givin' us 'is fish!

CAPTAIN. Well, there's nothin' for it but tote the things and walk till we get a lift.

WIFE. Oh! my corns are shootin'. I can't walk.

CAPTAIN. Cheerio, ma'am! Be English.

SHOPKEEPER. English! 'Tisn't *your* car.

CAPTAIN. Don't worry, old sport. 'E'll leave that in a ditch when he gets there.

SHOPKEEPER. There—ye-es—John o' Groats?

CAPTAIN. Come along, ma'am. Lift your corns well up. I'll give you a tune.

[*They have picked up the gear and are trailing off Right, leaving papers strewn about.*

WIFE. Oh! Look! We've left 'is fish.

SISTER. Fish! Infra dig, I call it. [*She sniffs.*

WIFE. Nonsense, Dolly! Dish of trout like that'll cost five shillings in Ashburton. May as well 'ave the worth of the petrol 'e'll use. Father, pick 'em up.

[*The* SHOPKEEPER *turns back, picks them up in the " Daily Mail," puts the combination to his nose, finds it good and follows the others off as the* CAPTAIN *begins to play his concertina and*

The curtain falls.

EPISODE VI

Half an hour has passed. An open space with the moor rising from it.

> [*A* MAN *in plus fours and his* WIFE *are returning from a walk. The* WIFE *has stopped and is moving her foot uneasily.*

WIFE. I've got something in my shoe, Philip.

MAN. What?

WIFE. I've got something in my shoe.

MAN. [*In front, stopping too*] Take it off, then. [*Goes back to her.*] Hold on to me.

WIFE. [*Taking off shoe and shaking it*] It isn't in the shoe—it's inside the stocking.

MAN. You can't sit down here; the ground's still wet.

WIFE. There—feel!

MAN. Yes, I can feel it.

WIFE. [*Standing on one leg*] Well! Hold me.

> [*He holds her and she has slipped her stocking off when there is the sound of an approaching car.*

MAN. Look out! Here's a car!

WIFE. [*Letting her skirt fall and standing on one leg*] Bother!
> [*Sound of the car stopping.*

MAN. Hallo! He's coming to speak to us.

> [*The* WIFE *bends and slips the shoe on hurriedly, but her dress is short. She holds the stocking behind her.*

MATT. [*Appearing*] Beg your pardon, sir, but can you direct me to Bovey?

MAN. Afraid we're strangers. Pity you didn't ask as you came through Widecombe.

MATT. Well, but it's up this hill, anyway, isn't it?

MAN. Must be, I think. That's the way to Heytor Rock.

MATT. Oh! Can you see the promised land from there?

WIFE. Yes.   You go up the hill and turn to the right, then to the left through a gate.

MATT. And ask again, I suppose. [*Preparing to leave.*] Thanks very much.

MAN. Fine place, the moor, sir.   Splendid air.

MATT. [*Dryly*] Oh! Splendid!   So dry and clear!

WIFE. [*With a giggle*] Yes, the fog *was* awful yesterday.

MAN. They say Bovey's pretty.

MATT. Yes, I've some Aunts there.   Good place for Aunts.

WIFE. [*Laughing*] What makes a good place for Aunts?

MATT. Oh! not too stirring.   Awfully good knitting there, I believe.

MAN. Ha!   That's good.   Ha!

MATT. I must get on, or I shall be late for tea.   So I whizz past Heytor rocks——?

WIFE. Yes, and come down on the church.

MATT. Thanks very much.   My Aunts are close there, I know.   Good afternoon.

> [*He lifts his hat discreetly and goes, Right.   The* MAN *and* WIFE *gaze after him.*

WIFE. What a nice young man!

MAN. That was good about Aunts. Ha! [*Sound of car moving on.*] Now for your stocking!

WIFE. [*Bending down and taking off her shoe*] I should think he was County, wouldn't you?

MAN. [*Holding her from behind*] Um!   Only "County" would drive such a shockin' bad car.

WIFE. He saw my leg and kept his eyes off it.   I thought that was charming of him.

MAN. Fellow-feelin'; he had some shockin' leg gear on himself.

WIFE. [*Turning stocking inside out*] See, there it is—a beastly little three-cornered bit of grit.   Extraordinary how they get in——

MAN. [*Suddenly*] Look out!   Here's a constable on a bike.

[*The* WIFE *drops her skirt and stands balancing again, the
    stocking in her hand. A very hot* CONSTABLE
    appears, wheeling a bicycle.

CONSTABLE. Zeen convict pass?

MAN. [*Astonished*] Convict? No.

CONSTABLE. Zeen anybody?

MAN. Only a car.

CONSTABLE. What zort of car?

MAN. Ford, I think.

CONSTABLE. Whu was in it?

MAN. A man.

CONSTABLE. What zort of man?

MAN. Oh!—er—a gentleman.

CONSTABLE. How d'yu know?

MAN. By his voice.

WIFE. He spoke to us.

CONSTABLE. What d'e zay?

MAN. Asked the way to Bovey.

CONSTABLE. Ha! What 'ad 'e on?

MAN. Long Burberry and a hat like mine; he was quite
all right.

CONSTABLE. [*Mopping his face*] Was 'e? Bovey—yu zay?

WIFE. Yes, he had some Aunts there—he was going to tea
with them.

CONSTABLE. [*Deeply*] Aunts in Bovey! Did yu direct
'im?

WIFE. We told him to go by Heytor rocks. Wasn't that
right?

CONSTABLE. Well, yu've directed the escaped convict.

MAN. [*Alarmed*] No, really! But I tell you——

WIFE. He was quite charming.

CONSTABLE. Was 'e? 'Ow much start's 'e got?

MAN. Oh! not five minutes. Of course, I didn't know—I
should never have——

CONSTABLE. [*Muttering and mopping*] This plaguey 'ill!

MAN. Hadn't you better telephone to Bovey?

CONSTABLE. [*Smartly*] Bovey! Why d'yu suppose he spoke to 'ee? Because 'e idn' goin' to Bovey and wants me to think 'e is.

WIFE. But really he was a gentleman.

CONSTABLE. [*Dryly*] Volk 'e stole that car from 'alf an hour gone, don't think so.   [*He mops his face.*

WIFE. I can't believe——

MAN. There were his legs.   [*To* CONSTABLE, *whose eyes are on the lady's leg.*] I noticed they looked like nothing at all.

CONSTABLE. Then why didn' yu stop 'im?

MAN. [*Flustered*] I would have, of course, if I'd suspected for a moment.

CONSTABLE. Stop first—suspect arterwards.

MAN. Well, I'm very sorry.   If I'd——

CONSTABLE. 'Tes done now.   I must get down along sharp and telephone.   [*He turns and wheels his bicycle off to the road.*

WIFE. [*On one leg*] I don't see why you need be sorry, Philip.   He *was* a gentleman.

MAN. A convict's a convict; you can't play about with the Law.

WIFE. Well, we have, that's one comfort.   That constable didn't keep *his* eyes off my leg.

MAN. I suppose you'd have had me get into a row with the police!

WIFE. Don't be silly, Philip!   You needn't get angry because your nerves are rattled.   No, don't hold me, I can put it on perfectly by myself.

[*She stands wobbling on one leg, and pulls the stocking on.*

MAN. The brass of that chap—talking about his Aunts!

WIFE. You thought it very funny, when he did.

MAN. If I'd known——

WIFE. Oh! Yes, if you'd known—you haven't an ounce of original sin in you.   Thank goodness, I have.

MAN. Where?   *I've* never——

WIFE. No, I don't keep it for you.

MAN. Hallo! He's coming back.

WIFE. Who? The constable?

MAN. No—that chap—the convict. [*Sounds of car.*

WIFE. Hooray!

MAN. What do you mean—hooray! What am I to do? This is infernal.

WIFE. [*Maliciously*] Run out and stop him, of course.

MAN. [*On one leg and the other*] He'd run over me. These chaps are desperate.

WIFE. Well, *I* will, then; and warn him of the constable.

MAN. You won't!—Hallo! He's stopping. That's worse. What the devil shall I do now?

[*The* WIFE *laughs. Sounds of car stopping.* MATT *reappears.*

MATT. Awfully sorry, but my car jibbed. There's another way round, isn't there? Through Widecombe, to the right— I saw a road?

MAN. Um! Well—I—er——

WIFE. Yes, but I shouldn't advise you to take it.

MATT. Must, I'm afraid. My car started to back down the hill.

MAN. I'm afraid—er—that I—er—ought to——

WIFE. My husband means that there's a constable in Wide-combe. [*Pointing.*

MATT. Yes. [*Looking back under his hand.*] I see him.

WIFE. So you'd better go on up.

MATT. There are *two* up there, you see. My car's very sensitive.

WIFE. Oh, dear!

MAN. Joan! [*Resolutely*] Now, sir, that constable's been talking to us. The game's up. If you don't mind, I'll take that car. He says it isn't yours.

MATT. [*Stepping back*] You know that's most frightfully true. But then—it isn't yours either.

MAN. Well, just let's argue it. I'm afraid you're helpless.

MATT. What do you take me for?

MAN. Why—er—the escaped convict, if you know what I mean.

MATT. Oh! Well—even so, I've still got a kick in me. I see your point of view, of course; but unfortunately I've got my own.

MAN. After that constable, I simply can't play about with it.

MATT. Look here! I've got a brain-wave. Let's all go into Widecombe in the car?

MAN. Ah! thanks very much; I thought you'd be sporting.

MATT. You see, if you're with me, I shall get through Widecombe all right, and I'll drop you just on the far side.

MAN. But——! What? No—that won't——

MATT. It's all right. You take me in custody into Widecombe—you can't help if it I whizz through and shoot you out. I want to make it easy for you, and I hope you want to make it easy for me.

MAN. Why should I? An escaped convict!

MATT. What do you call *yourself*?

MAN. What! Just an average man.

MATT. D'you mean to say the average man isn't a sportsman?

MAN. Yes. But I've had warning. I'm up against it.

WIFE. *I'll* come in the car. If you're with a lady, you'll get through without being spotted.

MATT. Splendid! Thanks ever so! Will you get in?

MAN. Joan!

MATT. Put yourself in my position, sir——

MAN. Look here! I ought to be knocking you down and sitting on your head, if you know what I mean.

MATT. [*Squaring up*] Well, any little thing you've got to do, please do it quickly.

MAN. Well, I mean—that's very crude.

WIFE. [*Ironically*] Oh! no, Philip! Oh, no!

MAN. Well, suppose you let me drive.

MATT. Why should I? I stole the car. Now, madam, shall we start?

WIFE. [*Winding her scarf round her face*] Right-o!

MAN. This is monstrous! Look here, sir, you seem to think——

MATT. I'll tell you what I think—[*Grimly*] I've been in purgatory too long, and I'm going to get out, and you're not going to stop me, if you know what I mean.

MAN. I jolly well am!

WIFE. Philip!

MAN. I'm not going to have it. If you won't surrender, I shall tackle you.

MATT. [*Dangerously*] Oh!

> [*He takes a spanner out of his pocket.*

WIFE. [*Stepping between them—to* MATT] D'you know, I think you'd better go on.

MATT. I think so, too. Sorry to be a boor and bring out a thing like this. [*Tapping the spanner.*] But I'm not playing, you see. [*Sombrely.*] The life we live spoils our sense of humour! Good-bye, ma'am, I'm very grateful to *you.*

> [*He turns and vanishes.*

MAN. Look here! You're not going like that—I'm damned if you are! Stop!

WIFE. Masterly, Philip! Masterly! [*Sound of a car starting.*] Run! My dear! Run! It's all right. You'll be too late.

MAN. You really *are*——

> [*They stand looking at each other as the sound of the car fails slowly, and*
>
> *The curtain falls.*

EPISODE VII

An hour has passed.

> [*In a gravel pit on the edge of the moor are a wheelbarrow, with a pick in it, and* MATT *lying on his face, apparently asleep, waiting for dark.*

> [*From Right comes the figure of a* LABOURER. *He is a burly great fellow with a shovel. Seeing the recumbent figure, he stands still, gazing. Then, turning, he goes back whence he came.* MATT, *who has been conscious of his visitor, gathers himself to spring up and rush away. Then he takes a resolution and lies down again in the same attitude, as if asleep. The* LABOURER *returns, followed by another* LABOURER *as big as himself. The* FIRST LABOURER *clears his throat.*

MATT. [*Sitting up with his feet under him*] Well, my men! What's the matter with you?

FIRST LABOURER. Beg pardon, zurr. We'm lukin' for th' escaped convict. We 'ad a zort of a thought as yu med be 'err.

MATT. Did you? That's pretty good! And now you see I'm not, suppose you apologize?

FIRST LABOURER. [*Cautiously*] 'Course, ef we knu 'u'm yu werr——

MATT. Whom do you work for?

FIRST LABOURER. Varmer Brownin'. 'Tes 'is grazin' yere.

MATT. I'll see Farmer Browning. It's funny, but I don't altogether like being taken for an escaped convict.

FIRST LABOURER. Yas, I rackon as 'ow yu'd better zee Maester Browning. George, goo and vind Maester. 'E'm in th' orchard long across.

> [*The* SECOND LABOURER *goes off, Left.*

FIRST LABOURER. We'm 'ad nues o' this joker, yu zee. Zeemingly 'e pinched a car and we'm found it just back along in the ditch. 'Tes the zame old car, tu.

MATT. What on earth's the car to do with me.

FIRST LABOURER. A don' zay nothin' 'bout that. Maester'll know when 'e comes.

MATT. I'll go and meet him.   [*He makes as if to rise.*

FIRST LABOURER. No, yu zett therr.

MATT. Now, look here, my friend! Do I talk like a convict?

FIRST LABOURER. Can't zay, never 'eerd none. They'm town folk, I rackon—mos'ly.

MATT. Well, I was bred in the country, like you. What wages do you get here?

> [*He pulls the flask out of his pocket, whistling " Lady, be good."*

FIRST LABOURER. Waal, ef yu'm the convict, yu'm a cule customer arter that.

MATT. But why on earth should you *think* I'm the convict? I'm just a fisherman staying at Lustleigh. [*He takes a pull at the empty flask.*] You're making a fool of yourself, you know.

FIRST LABOURER. [*Scratching his head*] Ef so be as yu'm what yu zay yu be, wot d'you goo vur to 'ide yere?

MATT. Hide? I was having a nap out of the wind, before walking home.

FIRST LABOURER. This joker 'ad a fishin-'rod wi' un, tu.

MATT. The convict? Bosh!

FIRST LABOURER. Not zo much bosh, neither.

MATT. Look you, my man, I've had enough of this.

> [*He stands up suddenly.*

> [*The* LABOURER *steps back and lifts his shovel. But at this moment the* FARMER *and* SECOND LABOURER *step into the picture from Left, accompanied by a* LITTLE GIRL *of thirteen or so, who has been riding.*

FARMER. Now then, now then! That'll du, Jim. Yu there, on my land, kindly give me yure name, and account for yureself. There's a rough customer about, with a fishin'-rod, same as yu.

MATT. Mr. Browning?

FARMER. Ay! that's my name.

MATT. Mine's Matthew. Captain Matthew. I'm staying at the Inn at Lustleigh. There's some very absurd mistake. This good trusty dog thinks he's treed a convict.

FARMER. [*Impressed by* MATT's *accent and air, and the flask in his hand*] Well, sir, when there's these escapes on the moor, we 'ave to be careful. Miss 'Lizabeth, yu run along.

    [*The* LITTLE GIRL *does not move, but remains spellbound.*] Constable's just been in wi' nues from Widecombe of the car yonder, and the man that pinched it 'ad a long brown coat, a fishin'-rod, and an 'at like yurn.

MATT. If the constable's here still, you'd better take me to him.

FARMER. No, rackon I'll ask 'im to step over 'ere. George, run and fetch constable, he'm down along by thiccy car.

    [*The* SECOND LABOURER *departs,* Right, *the* FIRST LABOURER *retires a little to the* Right, *leaving the* FARMER *and* MATT *by themselves on the* Left, *the* FARMER *being on the outside. The* LITTLE GIRL *still lurks breathless.*

MATT. Now, Mr. Browning—dash it all!—you ought to know better than this!

FARMER. Oh! I daresay yu'm a gentleman, but so's this convict, seemin'ly. Leastways he'm a captain. Perhaps yu'll tell me the name o' the innkeeper where yu'm stayin' at Lustleigh?

MATT. Has he got a name? I hadn't noticed.

FARMER. No; nor the name of the Inn neither, maybe?

MATT. The Red Lion.

FARMER. Ha!

MATT. Well, it ought to be.

FARMER. And per'aps yu'll show me the clothes yu've got on.

MATT. [*Taking a resolution*] Well, I own up.

LITTLE GIRL. Oh!

FARMER. I thowt yu'd come to it.

MATT. [*Lowering his voice*] Be sporting. Give me a show!

FARMER. Now yu know I can't du that; what's the yuse of askin'?

MATT. Well, I've had forty-eight hours' freedom, and given them a good run. You haven't a cigarette?

FARMER. I don't smoke them things. Jim, got a fag for this gentleman?

> [FIRST LABOURER *brings out a packet of cigarettes which he holds out. MATT takes one and lights it from a match sheltered in the horny hands of the LABOURER, who then retires again, Right, with the shovel.*

MATT. Thanks very much!   [*He sits on the wheelbarrow.*

> [*There ensues a silence. The* LITTLE GIRL *steals up to* MATT.

LITTLE GIRL. [*Holding out a small book*] Would you mind giving me your autograph?

FARMER. Miss 'Lizabeth!

LITTLE GIRL. Well, I've only just begun—I *have* to ask anybody at all thrilling.

MATT. [*With a grin*] Ink or—blood?

LITTLE GIRL. Oh! that'd be splendid!

MATT. Mine or—yours?

LITTLE GIRL. Oh! I've got a fountain pen. [*Hands it.* MATT *writes his name.*] Thank you so much.

MATT. [*Handing back the book*] Shake hands on it.

> [*The* LITTLE GIRL *and he shake hands.*]

When you're an old woman you'll be able to say you met Murderous Matt.—Mr. Browning, you won't give me a chance?

FARMER. Aid and abet a convict? No, no, Captain!

MATT. Vermin, eh? [*Looking round him.*] Well, you see, I've gone to earth. D'you hold with digging foxes out?

FARMER. I do, the varmints!

MATT. Ah! Well, you may thank your stars you were never in prison.

FARMER. No, an' I 'ope I'll never du nothin' to putt me there.

MATT. Take care you don't have bad luck, that's all.

FARMER. Bad luck? I rackon a man as kills a man can think he's havin' *gude* luck if he don't swing for it.

MATT. [*Sombrely*] I meant the poor beggar no harm.

LITTLE GIRL. Have you really killed a man?

MATT. Not yet.

FARMER. [*Removing the pick from the barrow*] Yu struck the blow, and he died of 't. What's more, so far as I remember, he was duin' his duty, same as I'm duin' mine.

> [*He looks intently at* MATT, *as if warning him not to try another blow.*

MATT. You needn't be afraid; there's a child here. If there weren't! I hope you'll see that my friend here [*Pointing to the* LABOURER] has the reward for my capture.

FARMER. 'E can 'ave it; I don' want no reward for duin' *my* duty.

MATT. [*Nodding gravely*] That's lucky! I appreciate your excellent intentions, Mr. Browning. Glad to have met you! Good-bye!

> [*He leaps from the barrow, and with a twist like a footballer evading a tackle, is past him and away to the Left. The* LITTLE GIRL *claps her hands.*

FARMER. [*Astonished*] The varmint! Hi! Jim! Arter 'im!

> [*The* LABOURER *utters a sort of roar and starts running. The* FARMER *is about to follow.*

LITTLE GIRL. Oh! Mr. Browning!

FARMER. Well?

LITTLE GIRL. Oh! nothing.

FARMER. Darn!   [*He follows out, running, Left.*

> [*The* CONSTABLE *and* SECOND LABOURER *come hurrying from Right.*

CONSTABLE. Gone! Which way, missy?

LITTLE GIRL. [*With distant blankness*] I don't know.

CONSTABLE. Come on, then!

> [*He and the* LABOURER *go out, Left, running.*

LITTLE GIRL. Oh! I do hope he gets off! Oh!

> [*On the hue and cry*
> *The curtain falls.*

EPISODE VIII

A few minutes have passed.

> [*In the parlour of a cottage of gentility are two maiden ladies*
> *—*MISS GRACE, *about forty-seven, brewing tea at a*
> *little table before the fire, Right, and* MISS DORA,
> *much younger, still dressed in hunting togs, standing*
> *at the open French window, Back.*

MISS DORA. There's such a glow on the Cleave, Grace. Most lovely red. We killed. Everybody was looking out for that escaped convict.

MISS GRACE. Did you see him?

MISS DORA. No, thank goodness. Poor hunted wretch!

MISS GRACE. If you think hunted things are poor, why do you go hunting?

MISS DORA. Foxes hunt and expect to be hunted.

MISS GRACE. So do convicts. Sympathy's wasted on them. Tea, Dora.

MISS DORA. This isn't a common convict. It's that Captain Denant, you remember——

MISS GRACE. Oh!—not likely to forget the row we had about his case! Well! it served him right!

MISS DORA. [*Going to the table and sitting down. Looking steadily at her sister*] For a good woman, Grace, you know—you're awfully hard.

MISS GRACE. Tea-cake, please. I like consistency.

MISS DORA. [*Deeply*] I think you're right.

MISS GRACE. [*Surprised*] How?

MISS DORA. It *is* a shame to hunt a fox—much better to shoot it.

MISS GRACE. There'd soon be no foxes. Don't get *that* bee into your bonnet *here*. What with rabbits, and chained dogs, you've set the farmers by the ears as it is. Wait till we go to Bath. You can have as many bees as you like there.

MISS DORA. I shan't hunt any more.

MISS GRACE. Then you're very foolish, if you enjoy it. Will you come over to the Service with me this evening?

MISS DORA. D'you know what I wish *you'd* say, Grace? "I shan't go to church any more."

MISS GRACE. I wish to God, Dora, you'd give up free thought!

MISS DORA. I wish to God, Grace, you'd give up religion.

MISS GRACE. You only hurt the vicar by it.

MISS DORA. [*Shaking her head*] He's too good a sort to mind.

MISS GRACE. You're too perverse for anything. I've only to say something and you set your will to the opposite.

MISS DORA. My dear, my will is nothing to yours. I haven't the ego for it.

MISS GRACE. [*Coldly*] You mean I'm egoistic? Thank you.

MISS DORA. Sorry, Grace.

MISS GRACE. Will you have another cup?

MISS DORA. Please.

> [*She is holding out her cup and* MISS GRACE *has poured from the teapot, when a Figure comes rushing through the French window. They both drop their hands and stare.* MATT, *panting and distressed, makes a sudden revealing gesture of appeal, and blots himself out behind a window curtain. The hue and cry is heard off. The two ladies are still staring in wild surprise, when the* FARMER *appears at the French window.*

FARMER. Which way d' 'e go?

MISS DORA. Who?

FARMER. Convict. Mun cam' over your waal un' round the corner ther'.

MISS DORA. Oh! Yes. I thought I saw. Across the lawn, and over the wall at the far end, Mr. Browning. Quick!

[*Behind her the figure and face of* MISS GRACE *are expressive.*

FARMER. Gude! Woi! Over the waal 'e went. To him, boys! Chop him before he'm into the spinney.

[*The hue and cry passes the window, running—the* TWO LABOURERS, *the* CONSTABLE, *and* TWO TOURIST YOUTHS. *The cries die off and leave a charged silence—the* TWO LADIES *on their feet.*

MATT. [*Emerging, still breathless, with his hat in his hand. Noting* MISS DORA'S *riding kit, he turns to* MISS GRACE] Thank you, madam.

MISS GRACE. Not me.

MATT. [*Making a bow to* MISS DORA] That was great of you, great!

MISS DORA. Keep back—one of them might see.

[*She draws the curtains as* MATT *shrinks back.*

MISS GRACE. Great! To tell such a lie! And for a convict!

MATT. [*Recovering his self-possession*] If you'll forgive my saying so, that makes it greater. To tell a lie for an archbishop wouldn't strain one a bit.

MISS GRACE. Please don't blaspheme.

MISS DORA. [*Pouring out tea*] Will you have a cup of tea, sir?

MISS GRACE. [*in a low voice*] Really, Dora!

MATT. [*Dropping his hat and taking the cup from* MISS DORA] It's too good of you. [*He drinks it straight off and hands it back.*] I'm most awfully sorry for butting in like this; but it was neck or nothing.

MISS GRACE. Then I think it should have been nothing, sir, considering the position you've placed my poor sister in.

MISS DORA. [*Hotly*] *Poor* sister! Grace, you——!

MATT. When you're hunted all you think of is the next move.

MISS DORA. I'm afraid you're awfully done.

MATT. Thanks, I'm getting my wind back. I feel like kissing the hem of your garment.

MISS DORA. It hasn't got one. Wasn't it rather mad to escape?

MATT. I don't think so. It's shown me how decent people can be.

MISS DORA. Did they ill-treat you?

MATT. Oh! no, the treatment's all right—a trifle monotonous.

MISS DORA. Listen!   [*They listen. Faint shouting.*] Where are you making for?

MATT. No plan. They're no good. It's like a battle— you change 'em before you use 'em.

MISS DORA. I read who you were in the papers.

MATT. Oh! yes. I'm in big print? Thank you most awfully. I'll clear out now.

MISS DORA. No, wait! [*At the curtains.*] I'll be back in a minute.   [*She slips out.*

MISS GRACE. [*Turning round to him*] I suppose you call yourself a gentleman?

MATT. I really don't know. Depends on who I'm with. I might be contradicted.

MISS GRACE. You see the sort of woman my sister is— impulsive, humanitarian. I'm—I'm very fond of her.

MATT. Naturally. She's splendid.

MISS GRACE. If you don't want to involve her——

MISS DORA. [*Reappearing through the curtains*] I think I can hide you.

MISS GRACE. Dora!

MATT. No, no! It's not good enough. I can't let you——

Miss Dora. [*Turning on her sister*] I'm going to, Grace.

[*They speak together in rapid tones.*

Miss Grace. Not in this house.

Miss Dora. It's as much my house as yours. You need have nothing to do with it.

Miss Grace. [*Drawing her from the window*] At least you haven't broken the law yet. And you're not going to now.

Miss Dora. I can't bear to see a soldier and a gentleman chased by a lot of chawbacons.

Miss Grace. [*With a glance at* Matt] Dora, you mustn't. It's wrong and it's absurd.

Miss Dora. [*Heated*] Go upstairs. If I have to refer to you, I'll say you've seen nothing. And so can you.

Miss Grace. [*Her voice rising*] You expect *me* to tell lies?

[Matt, *unseen in the heat of this discussion, makes a motion of despair and slips out of the window.*

Miss Dora. I'm going to hide him, I tell you. Captain—
[*Suddenly turning to* Matt, *she sees that he is no longer there.*]
Where is he?

[*The* Two Sisters *stand silent, blankly gazing about them.*

Miss Dora. Did he go by the door or the window?

Miss Grace. I don't know.

Miss Dora. Didn't you see him?

Miss Grace. I did not. [*At the expression on her sister's face.*] I say I did not.

[Miss Dora *looks behind the window curtain, then cautiously out of the window, then recoils before the* Constable, *who comes in heated and breathless, followed by the* Farmer *and the* First Labourer, *who stops outside.*

Constable. Beg pardon, miss. We've lost 'un. He'm a fair twister. Maybe he doubled back. We'll 'ave a luke over, if an' in case he'm hidin' yere somewhere about. Can we go thru yere?

Miss Dora. He can't be in the house.

[Miss Grace *stands pursing her lips.*

Farmer. We med 'ave a luke, miss, after that. 'E'm a proper varmint.

[*Without waiting for further permission, the two pass through the room and go out, Left. The* Two Sisters *stand looking at each other.*

Miss Dora. I won't have him caught!

[*She moves towards the door.*

Miss Grace. [*Seizing her sister's skirt*] Stop! I tell you!

Miss Dora. Let go!

Miss Grace. I shall not. You're crazy. What is it to you?

Miss Dora. Let go, Grace!

Miss Grace. You can't help him without breaking the law.

Miss Dora. Will you let me go, Grace? I shall hit you.

Miss Grace. Very well. Hit me, then!

[*The* Two Sisters *clinch, and for a moment it looks as if there were to be a physical struggle between them. There are sounds of approach.*

Miss Dora. Let go!

[*They unclinch, and wait for the door to open. Re-enter the* Farmer *and* Constable.

Farmer. Well, he'm not yere; that's certain for zure.

Constable. [*Between the two*] You're quite sure, miss, yu saw 'im over that wall?   [*A tense moment.*

Miss Dora. Quite!

[Miss Grace *has drawn her breath in with a hiss.*

Farmer. And not seen un since?

Miss Dora. No.

Farmer. Nor yu, miss?   [Miss Dora *stares at her sister.*

Miss Grace. [*Throwing up her head, and with a face like a mask*] No.

Farmer. [*Picking up* Matt's *hat, left by him as he fled*] 'Ere, what's this?

Miss Dora. [*Recovering*] That? An old hat of my brother's that I use sometimes.

Farmer. 'Tis uncommon like the one that varmint was wearin'.

Miss Dora. Is it? Those fishing hats are all the same. [*Taking the hat.*] Have you tried the orchard, Mr. Browning?

Farmer. Ah! we mun try that, but 'tis gettin' powerful dimsy. Come, boys, we mun 'ave a gude old luke. The varmint fuled me bravely. I mun get me own back.

Miss Dora. Try the vicarage!

Constable. Ah! we'll try that tu.

[*They pass out at the window.*
[*The* Two Sisters *are left silent.* Miss Grace *suddenly sits down at the table and covers her face with her hand.*

Miss Dora. You told it beautifully, Grace. Thank you!

Miss Grace. [*Uncovering her face with a fierce gesture*] Thank me for telling a lie!

Miss Dora. I'm sorry.

Miss Grace. Sorry? You'd make me do it again!

Miss Dora. [*Simply*] I would. [*Looking after the hunt.*] Poor fellow!   [*On the look between them*
                                        The curtain falls.

EPISODE IX

No time has passed. In the vestry of a village church lighted by an oil lamp, where, at the back, surplices and cassocks are hanging on pegs, a door, Right, leads to the churchyard and an open door, Left, into the church. There is no furniture except a chair or two, and a small table with a jug on it against the wall " up " from the door, Left.

[*The stage is empty, but almost at once the* Parson *enters from the church, carrying some overpast Harvest decorations, which he places on the table. He is a*

c

*slim, grizzle-haired, brown, active, middle-aged man
with a good, clean-shaven face, and a black Norfolk
jacket; obviously a little " High" in his doctrine.
He pours water from a jug into two large vases, hum-
ming: " O for the wings—for the wings of a
dove!" Then carrying the vases, one in each hand,
he goes back into the church. The door on the Right
is opened and the hunted, hatless* MATT *slips in,
closing the door behind him. He stands taking in the
situation, crosses to the open door opposite, spies the*
PARSON, *and, recoiling, blots himself out behind a
cassock. His face, peeping out, is withdrawn as the*
PARSON *returns, this time literally singing: " O for
the wings—for the wings of a dove!" Taking
off his coat, he prepares to hang it on a peg and take a
cassock, and as he reaches the highest note, he lifts
the cassock from in front of* MATT *and starts back.*

PARSON. Hullo!

MATT. Sanctuary, sir!

PARSON. What d'you mean? Who are you?

[MATT *opens his Burberry.*]

Oh! [*That " Oh!" is something more than astonishment; it
has in it an accent of dismay, as if the speaker were confronted by
his own soul.*] The escaped convict! You oughtn't to have
come in here.

MATT. Then where, sir? In old days the Church——

PARSON. In old days the Church was a thing apart; now
it belongs to the State.

[MATT *makes a move towards the door.*]

Wait a minute! [*He has hung up his coat and put on the cassock,
as if to strengthen the priest within him.*] I think I read that
you were that Captain Denant who——

MATT. Yes.

PARSON. [*Almost to himself*] Poor fellow!

[MATT *stares at him and there is a silence.*

MATT. Death isn't as much to us who were in the war, as it is to you.

PARSON. I know; I was there.

MATT. Padre?

PARSON. [*Nodding*] Where have you come from?

MATT. House of the two ladies over there. Left them fighting over me. Couldn't stand that—not worth it.

PARSON. [*With a little smile*] Yes, Miss Dora wanted to keep you and Miss Grace to throw you out. H'm? And yet Miss Dora doesn't come to church, and Miss Grace does. Something wrong there; or is it something right? [*He stares at* MATT.] Are they after you?

MATT. Full cry.

PARSON. Sanctuary? If I were a Roman. Sometimes wish I were.

MATT. More logical.

PARSON. More powerful. This is a situation I've never had to face, Captain Denant.

MATT. Well, sir, I'm just about done. If you could let me rest a bit, that's all I ask.

PARSON. My dear fellow! Sit down! [*He pulls a chair forward.*] I'll lock the door. [*He does so; then, as* MATT *looks up at the window, which is in the fourth wall.*] No, they can't see in. I expect you're very hungry, too.

MATT. [*Sitting*] No, thanks—beyond it. You know that feeling, I bet?

PARSON. [*Shaking his head.*] I'm afraid we of the Church lead too regular lives.

MATT. Not at the Front? It was pretty rife *there*.

PARSON. No, I'm ashamed to say—not even there.

[*While speaking, he is evidently pondering and torn.*

MATT. [*Suddenly*] Well, Padre, how does it look to you? Giving me up?

PARSON. [*Moved*] Padre! [*He takes a turn and comes to a sudden halt in front of* MATT'S *chair.*] As man to man—who am

I to give you up? One poor fellow to another! [*Shaking his head.*] I can't help you to escape, but if you want rest, take it.

MATT. [*Suddenly*] Wonder what Christ would have done!

PARSON. [*Gravely*] That, Captain Denant, is the hardest question in the world. Nobody ever knows. You may answer this or that, but nobody ever knows. The more you read those writings, the more you realize that He was incalculable. You see—He was a genius! It makes it hard for us who try to follow him. [*Gazing at* MATT, *who is sitting forward with his elbows on his knees and his head on his hands.*] Very tired?

MATT. Gosh! I didn't think one could feel so tired. My joints have gone on strike. I was a three-mile runner, too.

PARSON. Were you? Good man!

MATT. It's the strain here. [*Touching his head.*] If they get me and I have to go back! Odd! I didn't feel it half as much when I was escaping from Germany.

PARSON. Did anyone see you come in here?

MATT. Can't have—they'd have been on my heels.

PARSON. Who's after you?

MATT. Villagers—and a constable.

PARSON. My villagers—and here am I——

MATT. [*Standing up*] By George, yes, Padre! It's too bad. I'll clear out.

PARSON. [*Putting his hand on his shoulder and pressing him back into the chair.*] No, no! Rest while you can. You've asked for sanctuary. I don't know that I've the right to turn you out of here. I don't know—anyway I can't. Take your time. I have a little brandy here. Sometimes we get a faint in church. [*He takes a bottle and a little glass from the corner cupboard.*] Drink it down.

MATT. [*Drinking it off. Pulling out the flask.*] I say—I wonder if you'd return *this* for me; it's empty—to that name and address. [*He takes a tailor-sewn label out of his pocket.*]

I ripped it off this Burberry.   You might say " with unending gratitude."   But please don't give that name away.

PARSON. No, no; I'll see to it. [*Pockets it.*] Tell me! What made you escape?

MATT. Stick a bob-cat in a cage and open the door by mistake; and see what happens. [*Looking at the* PARSON'*s face.*] Oh! Yes, I know what you mean—but I've paid my scot long ago.

PARSON. Didn't you have a fair trial?

MATT. You can't " try " bad luck.

PARSON. All bad luck?

MATT. Well, I oughtn't to have hit him, of course; original sin, you know; but for an ordinary knock-out six weeks is about all you'd get; and I got four years more for that Rotten Row rail.   Yes, I think I was perfectly entitled to have a shot.

PARSON. If you're quiet in your own mind—that's the only thing.

MATT. Well, you needn't worry, Padre.   I shall be caught all right.

PARSON. [*With a smile*] I'm not worrying about that. Cæsar can look after himself, he has the habit.   What bothers me is my own peace of mind.   I don't like the thoughts that keep rising in it.   You led a company in the war.   And I lead——

MATT. Your parishioners—um?

PARSON. Yes. [*Nodding*] When you're gone—shall I be entitled to have been silent about you without telling *them* that I have been silent?   Am I entitled to refrain from helping the Law without letting *them* know it?   If I let them know it, can I keep what little influence I now possess?   And is it right for a parson to go on where he has no influence?   That's my trouble, Captain Denant.

MATT. I see. [*With a start.*] Someone's trying the door.

[*The* PARSON *moves to the door, Right ;* MATT *has started forward.*

PARSON. [*At the door*] Who is that?

VOICE OF BELLRINGER. Me, zurr.

PARSON. No, Thomas, I'm busy; I can't let anyone into the church now till Service time.   [*He stands listening, then returns, Centre.*] My bellringer.

MATT. [*In a low voice*] The hospitality of God—I shan't forget, Padre.   But I don't want to be on your conscience. I'll flit.   Wish I had the wings of that dove, though!

PARSON. I have Service at half-past six.   There will only be one or two gathered together, I'm afraid.   Make a third. You can rest through the Service.   No one comes in here.

MATT. You're a trump!   But I'd rather go and take my chance again.   It's dark now.   I don't like to give in.   I'll bolt, and be caught in the open.   You might give me your blessing.

PARSON. [*Shaking his head*] Not certain enough of myself— not certain enough.   It takes a bishop at least to give a blessing.

[*A very loud knocking on the door.*

MATT. Trapped, by George!

[*He springs towards the cassocks and blots himself out.*
[*The* PARSON *has gone again to the door.*

PARSON. [*Rather sharply*] What is that?

VOICE OF CONSTABLE. Open the door, zurr, please!

PARSON. Who is it?

VOICE OF CONSTABLE. Constable, zurr; open, please.

[*The* PARSON, *with a gesture of distress, opens the door.
Enter the* CONSTABLE, *the* FARMER, *the* TWO
LABOURERS, *and the* BELLRINGER.

PARSON. I told you, Thomas, I could see no one till after Service.

BELLRINGER. Yes, zurr; but Constable 'e thought you ought to know as 'ow I zeed a man enter 'ere a while back.

[*He looks round.*

PARSON. What's all this, Constable?

CONSTABLE. 'Tis th' escaped convict, zurr.   We'm after 'e.

These tu men yere found 'e down to the old gravel-pit.
'E give 'em the slip, an' we chased un to the ladies' 'ouse
yonder, wherr 'e gave us the goo-by again; and Tammas
says 'e saw a man come in 'ere as sounds praaperly like the
varmint.   You ben 'ere long, zurr?

PARSON. An hour, at least.

CONSTABLE. Front door's locked, but I got men in the
porch.   Be 'ee sure as there's no one in the church?

PARSON. [*Moving towards the church door*] I don't know
whether you have the right to search a holy place; but look
for yourselves, as quietly as you can, please.

> [*He stands at the church door to let them pass.*
> [*They go, with the exception of the* BELLRINGER, *who has re-
> mained by the vestry door.   The* PARSON *crosses to him.*

You can go too, Thomas.   I'll stand here.

> [*The* BELLRINGER, *with uneasy eyes and motions, crosses
> under the compulsion of the* PARSON's *glance.*

PARSON. [*Hardly moving his lips*] Now, quick!

> [*But as he speaks, the* FARMER *reappears in the church door-
> way;   the* PARSON *has just time to make a warning
> gesture,* MATT *just time to blot himself out again.*

PARSON. Well, Browning?

FARMER. 'Eem not therr; 'tes zo bare's me 'and.   'Eem a
proper twisty customer for sure, but we'll get 'e yet.

> [*His eyes rest suspiciously on the* PARSON's *face.*

PARSON. [*With a forced smile*] He got away from you, then,
did he?

FARMER. Aye!   'E can run an' twist like a rabbit.   He'm a
desperate foxy chap.   What's behind they cassocks?

PARSON. [*Still with that forced smile*] I'll look, Browning.

> [*He moves to the cassocks, and, from the middle, takes a
> look behind them, but to the Left only.   And at this mo-
> ment they all return from the church and he turns to them.*

CONSTABLE. Thank 'ee, zurr;   'e'm not yere, Tammas.
Yu made a fule of us zeemin'ly.

BELLRINGER. [*Stammering*] I zeed mun come in 'ere; I zeed mun wi' these eyes—I did zurely.

PARSON. [*Looking at his watch*] Service, Thomas. Go and ring the bell.   [*To the* CONSTABLE.] I'm afraid I must ask you to go too, please, unless you would all like to stay for Service.   [*A certain length of face becomes apparent.*

CONSTABLE. [*Opening the door and beckoning the* MEN *out*] My juty, zurr, ef yu'll excuse us.

PARSON. That's all right, Constable.

FARMER. [*Suddenly*] Jest a minute, Vicar. Yu'll pardon me askin', but are yo zartun zure as yu'm not zeen this joker?

PARSON. [*Drawing himself up*] What is it you are asking me?

FARMER. I'm askin' yu on yure honour as a Christian gentleman, whether or no yu've zeen the escaped convict?

[*After a moment's intense silence.*

PARSON. I——

MATT. [*Stepping out without the Burberry*] Certainly he's not.   Sorry, sir, I was hidden there. [*Holding up his hands.*] I surrender, Constable.

FARMER. Woi! The varmint! Got un! Worry, worry, worry!

PARSON. Be quiet in this place; and go out—You shame God!

[*Astonished at this outburst, they slink out, leaving* MATT, *Centre, in the grip of the* CONSTABLE. *The* PARSON *is on his Left.*

MATT. [*To the* PARSON] Forgive me, sir! Oughtn't to have come in here.   It wasn't playing cricket.

PARSON. No, no! That you *have* done—that you *have* done.

MATT. It's one's decent *self* one can't escape.

PARSON. Ah! that's it! [*Very low.*] God keep you!

[*He watches the* CONSTABLE *and* MATT *go out. The bell begins to ring, as*
                    The curtain falls.

THE ELDEST SON

PERSONS OF THE PLAY

SIR WILLIAM CHESHIRE, *a baronet*
LADY CHESHIRE, *his wife*
BILL, *their eldest son*
HAROLD, *their second son*
RONALD KEITH (*in the Lancers*), *their son-in-law*
CHRISTINE (*his wife*), *their eldest daughter*
DOT, *their second daughter*
JOAN, *their third daughter*
MABEL LANFARNE, *their guest*
THE REVEREND JOHN LATTER, *engaged to Joan*
OLD STUDDENHAM, *the head-keeper*
FREDA STUDDENHAM, *the lady's-maid*
YOUNG DUNNING, *the under-keeper*
ROSE TAYLOR, *a village girl*
JACKSON, *the butler*
CHARLES, *a footman*

TIME: *The present. The action passes on December 7 and 8 at the Cheshires' country house, in one of the shires.*

ACT I., SCENE I. *The hall; before dinner.*
      SCENE II. *The hall; after dinner.*

ACT II. *Lady Cheshire's morning-room; after breakfast.*

ACT III. *The smoking-room; tea-time.*

A night elapses between Acts I. and II.

ACT I

SCENE I

The scene is a well-lighted, and large, oak-panelled hall, with an air of being lived in, and a broad, oak staircase.   The dining-room, drawing-room, billiard-room, all open into it ; and under the staircase a door leads to the servants' quarters.   In a huge fireplace a log fire is burning.   There are tiger-skins on the floor, horns on the walls ; and a writing-table against the wall opposite the fireplace.   FREDA STUDDENHAM, a pretty, pale girl with dark eyes, in the black dress of a lady's-maid, is standing at the foot of the staircase with a bunch of white roses in one hand, and a bunch of yellow roses in the other.   A door closes above, and SIR WILLIAM CHESHIRE, in evening dress, comes downstairs.   He is perhaps fifty-eight, of strong build, rather bull-necked, with grey eyes, and a well-coloured face, whose choleric autocracy is veiled by a thin urbanity.   He speaks before he reaches the bottom.

SIR WILLIAM. Well, Freda ! Nice roses. Who are they for ?

FREDA. My lady told me to give the yellow to Mrs. Keith, Sir William, and the white to Miss Lanfarne, for their first evening.

SIR WILLIAM. Capital. [*Passing on towards the drawing-room.*] Your father coming up to-night ?

FREDA. Yes.

SIR WILLIAM. Be good enough to tell him I specially want to see him here after dinner, will you ?

FREDA. Yes, Sir William.

SIR WILLIAM. By the way, just ask him to bring the game-book in, if he's got it.

> [*He goes out into the drawing-room; and* FREDA *stands restlessly tapping her foot against the bottom stair. With a flutter of skirts* CHRISTINE KEITH *comes rapidly down. She is a nice-looking, fresh-coloured young woman in a low-necked dress.*

CHRISTINE. Hullo, Freda! How are *you*?

FREDA. Quite well, thank you, Miss Christine—Mrs. Keith, I mean. My lady told me to give you these.

CHRISTINE. [*Taking the roses*] Oh! Thanks! How sweet of mother!

FREDA. [*In a quick toneless voice*] The others are for Miss Lanfarne. My lady thought white would suit her better.

CHRISTINE. They suit *you* in that black dress.

> [FREDA *lowers the roses quickly.*]

What do you think of Joan's engagement?

FREDA. It's very nice for her.

CHRISTINE. I say, Freda, have they been going hard at rehearsals?

FREDA. Every day. Miss Dot gets very cross, stage-managing.

CHRISTINE. I do hate learning a part. Thanks awfully for unpacking. Any news?

FREDA. [*In the same quick, dull voice*] The under-keeper, Dunning, won't marry Rose Taylor, after all.

CHRISTINE. What a shame! But I say that's serious. I thought there was—she was—I mean——

FREDA. He's taken up with another girl, they say.

CHRISTINE. Too bad! [*Pinning the roses.*] D'you know if Mr. Bill's come?

FREDA. [*With a swift upward look*] Yes, by the six-forty.

> [RONALD KEITH *comes slowly down, a weathered firm-lipped man, in evening dress, with eyelids half drawn over his keen eyes, and the air of a horseman.*

KEITH. Hallo! Roses in December. I say, Freda, your father missed a wigging this morning when they drew blank at Warnham's spinney. Where's that litter of little foxes?

FREDA. [*Smiling faintly*] I expect father knows, Captain Keith.

KEITH. You bet he does. Emigration? Or thin air? What?

CHRISTINE. Studdenham'd never shoot a fox, Ronny. He's been here since the flood.

KEITH. There's more ways of killing a cat—eh, Freda?

CHRISTINE. [*Moving with her husband towards the drawing-room*] Young Dunning won't marry that girl, Ronny.

KEITH. Phew! Wouldn't be in his shoes, then! Sir William'll never keep a servant who's made a scandal in the village. Bill come?

> [*As they disappear from the hall,* JOHN LATTER, *in a clergyman's evening dress, comes sedately downstairs, a tall, rather pale young man, with something in him, as it were, both of heaven and a drawing-room. He passes* FREDA *with a formal little nod.* HAROLD, *a fresh-cheeked, cheery-looking youth, comes down, three steps at a time.*

HAROLD. Hallo, Freda! Patience on the monument. Let's have a sniff! For Miss Lanfarne? Bill come down yet?

FREDA. No, Mr. Harold.

> [HAROLD *crosses the hall, whistling, and follows* LATTER *into the drawing-room. There is the sound of a scuffle above, and a voice crying:* " Shut up, Dot! " *And* JOAN *comes down screwing her head back. She is pretty and small, with large clinging eyes.*

JOAN. Am I all right behind, Freda? That beast, Dot!

FREDA. Quite, Miss Joan.

> [DOT'S *face, like a full moon, appears over the upper banisters. She too comes running down, a frank figure, with a face of a rebel.*

DOT. You little *being* !

JOAN. [*Flying towards the drawing-room, is overtaken at the door*] Oh! Dot! You're pinching!

> [*As they disappear into the drawing-room,* MABEL LAN-
> FARNE, *a tall girl with a rather charming Irish face,
> comes slowly down. And at sight of her* FREDA'S
> *whole figure becomes set and meaning-full.*

FREDA. For you, Miss Lanfarne, from my lady.

MABEL. [*In whose speech is a touch of wilful Irishry*] How sweet! [*Fastening the roses.*] And how are *you*, Freda?

FREDA. Very well, thank you.

MABEL. And your father? Hope he's going to let me come out with the guns again.

FREDA. [*Stolidly*] He'll be delighted, I'm sure.

MABEL. Ye-es! I haven't forgotten his face—last time.

FREDA. You stood with Mr. Bill. He's better to stand with than Mr. Harold, or Captain Keith?

MABEL. He didn't touch a feather, that day.

FREDA. People don't when they're anxious to do their best.

> [*A gong sounds. And* MABEL LANFARNE, *giving* FREDA *a
> rather inquisitive stare, moves on to the drawing-room.
> Left alone without the roses,* FREDA *still lingers. At
> the slamming of a door above, and hasty footsteps, she
> shrinks back against the stairs.* BILL *runs down,
> and comes on her suddenly. He is a tall, good-looking
> edition of his father, with the same stubborn look of
> veiled choler.*

BILL. Freda! [*And as she shrinks still further back.*] What's the matter? [*Then at some sound he looks round uneasily and draws away from her.*] Aren't you glad to see me?

FREDA. I've something to say to you, Mr. Bill. After dinner.

BILL. Mister——?

> [*She passes him, and rushes away upstairs. And* BILL, *who
> stands frowning and looking after her, recovers himself*

sharply as the drawing-room door is opened, and SIR
WILLIAM *and* MISS LANFARNE *come forth, followed
by* KEITH, DOT, HAROLD, CHRISTINE, LATTER, *and*
JOAN, *all leaning across each other, and talking. By
herself, behind them, comes* LADY CHESHIRE, *a
refined-looking woman of fifty, with silvery dark hair,
and an expression at once gentle and ironic. They
move across the hall towards the dining-room.*

SIR WILLIAM. Ah! Bill.

MABEL. How do you do?

KEITH. How are you, old chap?

DOT. [*Gloomily*] Do you know your part?

HAROLD. Hallo, old man!

[CHRISTINE *gives her brother a flying kiss.* JOAN *and*
LATTER *pause and look at him shyly without speech.*

BILL. [*Putting his hand on* JOAN'S *shoulder*] Good luck, you
two! Well, mother?

LADY CHESHIRE. Well, my dear boy! Nice to see you at
last. What a long time!

[*She draws his arm through hers, and they move towards
the dining-room.*

The curtain falls.
The curtain rises again at once.

SCENE II

CHRISTINE, LADY CHESHIRE, DOT, MABEL LANFARNE, *and* JOAN
are returning to the hall after dinner.

CHRISTINE. [*In a low voice*] Mother, is it true about young
Dunning and Rose Taylor?

LADY CHESHIRE. I'm afraid so, dear.

CHRISTINE. But can't they be——

DOT. Ah! ah-h! [CHRISTINE *and her mother are silent.*]
My child, I'm not the young person.

CHRISTINE. No, of course not—only—[*nodding towards* JOAN *and* MABEL].

DOT. Look here! This is just an instance of what I hate.

LADY CHESHIRE. My dear? Another one?

DOT. Yes, mother, and don't you pretend you don't understand, because you know you do.

CHRISTINE. Instance? Of what?

[JOAN *and* MABEL *have ceased talking, and listen, still at the fire.*]

DOT. Humbug, of course. Why should you want them to marry, if he's tired of her?

CHRISTINE. [*Ironically*] Well! If your imagination doesn't carry you as far as that!

DOT. When people marry, do you believe they ought to be in love with each other?

CHRISTINE. [*With a shrug*] That's not the point.

DOT. Oh? Were you in love with Ronny?

CHRISTINE. Don't be idiotic!

DOT. Would you have married him if you hadn't been?

CHRISTINE. Of course not!

JOAN. Dot! You are!——

DOT. Hallo! my little snipe!

LADY CHESHIRE. Dot, dear!

DOT. Don't shut me up, mother! [*To* JOAN.] Are you in love with John? [JOAN *turns hurriedly to the fire.*] Would you be going to marry him if you were not?

CHRISTINE. You are a brute, Dot.

DOT. Is Mabel in love with—whoever she is in love with?

MABEL. And I wonder who that is.

DOT. Well, would you marry him if you weren't?

MABEL. No, I would *not*.

DOT. Now, mother; did you love father?

CHRISTINE. Dot, you really are awful.

DOT. [*Rueful and detached*] Well, it is a bit too thick, perhaps.

JOAN. Dot!

DOT. Well, mother, did you—I mean quite calmly?

LADY CHESHIRE. Yes, dear, quite calmly.

DOT. Would you have married him if you hadn't? [LADY CHESHIRE *shakes her head.*] Then we're all agreed!

MABEL. Except yourself.

DOT. [*Grimly*] Even if I loved him, he might think himself lucky if I married him.

MABEL. Indeed, and I'm not so sure.

DOT. [*Making a face at her*] What I was going to——

LADY CHESHIRE. But don't you think, dear, you'd better not?

DOT. Well, I won't say what I was going to say, but what I do say is—Why the devil——

LADY CHESHIRE. Quite so, Dot!

DOT. [*A little disconcerted*] If they're tired of each other, they ought not to marry, and if father's going to make them——

CHRISTINE. You don't understand in the least. It's for the sake of the——

DOT. Out with it, Old Sweetness! The approaching infant! God bless it!

> [*There is a sudden silence, for* KEITH *and* LATTER *are seen coming from the dining-room.*

LATTER. That must be so, Ronny.

KEITH. No, John; not a bit of it!

LATTER. You don't *think* !

KEITH. Good Gad, who wants to think after dinner!

DOT. Come on! Let's play Pool. [*She turns at the billiard-room door.*] Look here! Rehearsal to-morrow is directly after breakfast; from " Eccles enters breathless " to the end.

MABEL. Whatever made you choose *Caste*, Dot? You know it's awfully difficult.

DOT. Because it's the only play that's not too advanced.

> [*The girls all go into the billiard-room.*

LADY CHESHIRE. Where's Bill, Ronny?

KEITH. [*With a grimace*] I rather think Sir William and he are in Committee of Supply—Mem-Sahib.

LADY CHESHIRE. Oh!

[*She looks uneasily at the dining-room; then follows the girls out.*

LATTER. [*In the tone of one resuming an argument*] There can't be two opinions about it, Ronny. Young Dunning's refusal is simply indefensible.

KEITH. I don't agree a bit, John.

LATTER. Of course, if you won't listen.

KEITH. [*Clipping a cigar*] Draw it mild, my dear chap. We've had the whole thing over twice at least.

LATTER. My point is this——

KEITH. [*Regarding* LATTER *quizzically with his half-closed eyes*] I know—I know—but the point is, how far your point is simply professional.

LATTER. If a man wrongs a woman, he ought to right her again. There's no answer to that.

KEITH. It all depends.

LATTER. That's rank opportunism.

KEITH. Rats! Look here—Oh! hang it, John, one can't argue this out with a parson.

LATTER. [*Frigidly*] Why not?

HAROLD. [*Who has entered from the dining-room*] Pull devil, pull baker!

KEITH. Shut up, Harold!

LATTER. "To play the game" is the religion even of the Army.

KEITH. Exactly, but what *is* the game?

LATTER. What else can it be in this case?

KEITH. You're too puritanical, young John. You can't help it—line of country laid down for you. All drag-huntin'! What!

LATTER. [*With concentration*] Look here!

HAROLD. [*Imitating the action of a man pulling at a horse's head*] "Come hup, I say, you hugly beast!"

KEITH. [*To* LATTER] You're not going to draw me, old chap. You don't see where you'd land us all. [*He smokes calmly.*]

LATTER. How do you imagine vice takes its rise? From precisely this sort of thing of young Dunning's.

KEITH. From human nature, I should have thought, John. I admit that I don't like a fellow's leavin' a girl in the lurch; but I don't see the use in drawin' hard and fast rules. You only have to break 'em. Sir William and you would just tie Dunning and the girl up together, willy-nilly, to save appearances, and ten to one but there'll be the deuce to pay in a year's time. You can take a horse to the water, you can't make him drink.

LATTER. I entirely and absolutely disagree with you.

HAROLD. Good old John!

LATTER. At all events we know where your principles take you.

KEITH. [*Rather dangerously*] Where, please? [HAROLD *turns up his eyes, and points downwards.*] Dry up, Harold!

LATTER. Did you ever hear the story of Faust?

KEITH. Now look here, John: with all due respect to your cloth, and all the politeness in the world, you may go to—blazes.

LATTER. Well, I must say, Ronny—of all the rude boors——   [*He turns towards the billiard-room.*

KEITH. Sorry I smashed the glass, old chap.

[LATTER *passes out. There comes a mingled sound through the opened door, of female voices, laughter, and the click of billiard balls, clipped off by the sudden closing of the door.*

KEITH. [*Impersonally*] Deuced odd, the way a parson puts one's back up! Because you know I agree with him really; young Dunning *ought* to play the game; and I hope Sir William 'll make him.

[*The butler* JACKSON *has entered from the door under the stairs followed by the keeper* STUDDENHAM, *a man between fifty and sixty, in a full-skirted coat with big pockets, cord breeches and gaiters; he has a steady self-respecting weathered face, with blue eyes and a short grey beard, which has obviously once been red.*

KEITH. Hullo! Studdenham!

STUDDENHAM. [*Touching his forehead*] Evenin', Captain Keith.

JACKSON. Sir William still in the dining-room with Mr. Bill, sir?

HAROLD. [*With a grimace*] He is, Jackson.

[JACKSON *goes out to the dining-room.*

KEITH. You've shot no pheasants yet, Studdenham?

STUDDENHAM. No, sir. Only birds. We'll be doin' the spinneys and the home covert while you're down.

KEITH. I say, talkin' of spinneys——

[*He breaks off sharply, and goes out with* HAROLD *into the billiard-room.* SIR WILLIAM *enters from the dining-room, applying a gold toothpick to his front teeth.*

SIR WILLIAM. Ah! Studdenham. Bad business this about young Dunning!

STUDDENHAM. Yes, Sir William.

SIR WILLIAM. He definitely refuses to marry her?

STUDDENHAM. He does that.

SIR WILLIAM. That won't do, you know. What reason does he give?

STUDDENHAM. Won't say other than that he don't want no more to do with her.

SIR WILLIAM. God bless me! That's not a reason. I can't have a keeper of mine playing fast and loose in the village like this. [*Turning to* LADY CHESHIRE, *who has come in from the billiard-room.*] That affair of young Dunning's, my dear.

LADY CHESHIRE. Oh! Yes! I'm *so* sorry, Studdenham. The poor girl!

STUDDENHAM. [*Respectfully*] Fancy he's got a feeling she's not his equal, now, my lady.

LADY CHESHIRE. [*To herself*] Yes, I suppose he *has* made her his superior.

SIR WILLIAM. What? Eh! Quite! Quite! I was just telling Studdenham the fellow must set the matter straight. We can't have open scandals in the village. If he wants to keep his place he must marry her at once.

LADY CHESHIRE. [*To her husband in a low voice*] Is it right to force them? Do you know what the girl wishes, Studdenham?

STUDDENHAM. Shows a spirit, my lady—says she'll have him—willin' or not.

LADY CHESHIRE. A spirit? I see. If they marry like that they're sure to be miserable.

SIR WILLIAM. What! Doesn't follow at all. Besides, my dear, you ought to know by this time, there's an unwritten law in these matters. They're perfectly well aware that when there are consequences, they have to take them.

STUDDENHAM. Some o' these young people, my lady, they don't put two and two together no more than an old cock pheasant.

SIR WILLIAM. I'll give him till to-morrow. If he remains obstinate, he'll have to go; he'll get no character, Studdenham. Let him know what I've said. I like the fellow, he's a good keeper. I don't want to lose him. But this sort of thing I won't have. He must toe the mark or take himself off. Is he up here to-night?

STUDDENHAM. Hangin' partridges, Sir William. Will you have him in?

SIR WILLIAM. [*Hesitating*] Yes—yes. I'll see him.

STUDDENHAM. Good-night to you, my lady.

LADY CHESHIRE. Freda's not looking well, Studdenham.

STUDDENHAM. She's a bit pernickitty with her food, that's where it is.

LADY CHESHIRE. I must try and make her eat.

SIR WILLIAM. Oh! Studdenham. We'll shoot the home covert first. What did we get last year?

STUDDENHAM. [*Producing the game-book; but without reference to it*] Two hundred and fifty-three pheasants, eleven hares, fifty-two rabbits, three woodcock, sundry.

SIR WILLIAM. Sundry? Didn't include a fox, did it? [*Gravely.*] I was seriously upset this morning at Warnham's spinney——

STUDDENHAM. [*Very gravely*] Yu don't say, Sir William; that four-year-old he du look a handful!

SIR WILLIAM. [*With a sharp look*] You know well enough what I mean.

STUDDENHAM. [*Unmoved*] Shall I send young Dunning, Sir William?

[SIR WILLIAM *gives a short, sharp nod, and* STUDDENHAM *retires by the door under the stairs.*]

SIR WILLIAM. Old fox!

LADY CHESHIRE. Don't be too hard on Dunning. He's very young.

SIR WILLIAM. [*Patting her arm*] My dear, you don't understand young fellows, how should you?

LADY CHESHIRE. [*With her faint irony*] A husband and two sons not counting. [*Then as the door under the stairs is opened.*] Bill, now do——

SIR WILLIAM. I'll be gentle with him. [*Sharply.*] Come in!

[LADY CHESHIRE *retires to the billiard-room. She gives a look back and a half smile at young* DUNNING, *a fair young man dressed in brown cords and leggings, and holding his cap in his hand; then goes out.*]

SIR WILLIAM. Evenin', Dunning.

DUNNING. [*Twisting his cap*] Evenin', Sir William.

SIR WILLIAM. Studdenham's told you what I want to see you about?

DUNNING. Yes, Sir.

SIR WILLIAM. The thing's in your hands. Take it or leave it. I don't put pressure on you. I simply won't have this sort of thing on my estate.

DUNNING. I'd like to say, Sir William, that she—— [*He stops.*]

SIR WILLIAM. Yes, I daresay—Six of one and half a dozen of the other. Can't go into that.

DUNNING. No, Sir William.

SIR WILLIAM. I'm quite mild with you. This is your first place. If you leave here you'll get no character.

DUNNING. I never meant any harm, sir.

SIR WILLIAM. My good fellow, you know the custom of the country.

DUNNING. Yes, Sir William, but——

SIR WILLIAM. You should have looked before you leaped. I'm not forcing you. If you refuse you must go, that's all.

DUNNING. Yes, Sir William.

SIR WILLIAM. Well, now go along and take a day to think it over.

> [BILL, *who has sauntered moodily from the dining-room, stands by the stairs listening. Catching sight of him,* DUNNING *raises his hand to his forelock.*

DUNNING. Very good, Sir William. [*He turns, fumbles, and turns again.*] My old mother's dependent on me——

SIR WILLIAM. Now, Dunning, I've no more to say.

> [DUNNING *goes sadly away under the stairs.*

SIR WILLIAM. [*Following*] And look here! Just understand this—— [*He too goes out.*

> [BILL, *lighting a cigarette, has approached the writing-table. He looks very grim. The billiard-room door is flung open.* MABEL LANFARNE *appears, and makes him a little curtsey.*

MABEL. Against my will I am bidden to bring you in to pool.

BILL. Sorry! I've got letters.

MABEL. You seem to have become very conscientious.

BILL. Oh! I don't know.

MABEL. Do you remember the last day of the covert shooting?

BILL. I do.

MABEL. [*Suddenly*] What a pretty girl Freda Studdenham's grown!

BILL. Has she?

MABEL. " She walks in beauty."

BILL. Really? Hadn't noticed.

MABEL. Have you been taking lessons in conversation?

BILL. Don't think so.

MABEL. Oh! [*There is a silence.*] Mr. Cheshire.

BILL. Miss Lanfarne!

MABEL. What's the matter with you? Aren't you rather queer, considering that I don't bite, and *was* rather a pal!

BILL. [*Stolidly*] I'm sorry.

> [*Then seeing that his mother has come in from the billiard-room, he sits down at the writing-table.*

LADY CHESHIRE. Mabel, dear, do take my cue. Won't you play too, Bill, and try and stop Ronny, he's too terrible?

BILL. Thanks. I've got these letters.

> [MABEL *taking the cue passes back into the billiard-room, whence comes out the sound of talk and laughter.*

LADY CHESHIRE. [*Going over and standing behind her son's chair*] Anything wrong, darling?

BILL. Nothing, thanks. [*Suddenly.*] I say, I wish you hadn't asked that girl here.

LADY CHESHIRE. Mabel! Why? She's wanted for rehearsals. I thought you got on so well with her last Christmas.

BILL. [*With a sort of sullen exasperation*] A year ago.

LADY CHESHIRE. The girls like her, so does your father; personally I must say I think she's rather nice and Irish.

BILL. She's all right, I daresay.

[*He looks round as if to show his mother that he wishes to be left alone. But* LADY CHESHIRE, *having seen that he is about to look at her, is not looking at him.*

LADY CHESHIRE. I'm afraid your father's been talking to you, Bill.

BILL. He has.

LADY CHESHIRE. Debts? Do try and make allowances. [*With a faint smile.*] Of course he is a little——

BILL. He is.

LADY CHESHIRE. I wish *I* could——

BILL. Oh, Lord! Don't *you* get mixed up in it!

LADY CHESHIRE. It seems almost a pity that you told him.

BILL. He wrote and asked me point-blank what I owed.

LADY CHESHIRE. Oh! [*Forcing herself to speak in a casual voice.*] I happen to have a little money, Bill—— I think it would be simpler if——

BILL. Now look here, mother, you've tried that before. I can't help spending money, I never *shall* be able, unless I go to the Colonies, or something of the kind.

LADY CHESHIRE. Don't talk like that!

BILL. I *would*, for two straws!

LADY CHESHIRE. It's only because your father thinks such a lot of the place, and the name, and your career. The Cheshires are all like that. They've been here so long; they're all—root.

BILL. Deuced funny business my career will be, I expect!

LADY CHESHIRE. [*Fluttering, but restraining herself lest he should see*] But, Bill, why *must* you spend more than your allowance?

BILL. Why—anything? I didn't make myself.

LADY CHESHIRE. I'm afraid *we* did that. It *was* inconsiderate perhaps.

BILL. Yes, you'd better have left me out.

LADY CHESHIRE. But why are you so—— Only a little fuss about money!

BILL. Ye-es.

LADY CHESHIRE. You're not keeping anything from me, are you?

BILL. [*Facing her*] No. [*He then turns very deliberately to the writing things, and takes up a pen.*] I must write these letters, please.

LADY CHESHIRE. Bill, if there's any real trouble, you will tell me, won't you?

BILL. There's nothing whatever.

[*He suddenly gets up and walks about.*

[LADY CHESHIRE, *too, moves over to the fireplace, and after an uneasy look at him, turns to the fire. Then, as if trying to switch off his mood, she changes the subject abruptly.*

LADY CHESHIRE. Isn't it a pity about young Dunning? I'm so sorry for Rose Taylor.

[*There is a silence. Stealthily under the staircase* FREDA *has entered, and seeing only* BILL, *advances to speak to him.*

BILL. [*Suddenly*] Oh! well, you can't help these things in the country.

[*As he speaks,* FREDA *stops dead, perceiving that he is not alone;* BILL, *too, catching sight of her, starts.*

LADY CHESHIRE. [*Still speaking to the fire*] It seems dreadful to force him. I do so believe in people doing things of their own accord. [*Then seeing* FREDA *standing so uncertainly by the stairs.*] Do you want me, Freda?

FREDA. Only your cloak, my lady. Shall I—begin it?

[*At this moment* SIR WILLIAM *enters from the drawing-room.*

LADY CHESHIRE. Yes, yes.

SIR WILLIAM. [*Genially*] Can you give me another five minutes, Bill? [*Pointing to the billiard-room.*] We'll come directly, my dear.

[FREDA, *with a look at* BILL, *has gone back whence she came; and* LADY CHESHIRE *goes reluctantly away into the billiard-room.*

Sir William. I shall give young Dunning short shrift. [*He moves over to the fireplace and divides his coat-tails.*] Now, about you, Bill! I don't want to bully you the moment you come down, but, you know, this can't go on. I've paid your debts twice. Shan't pay them this time unless I see a disposition to change your mode of life. [*A pause.*] You get your extravagance from your mother. She's very queer—[*A pause.*]—All the Winterleghs are like that about money.

Bill. Mother's particularly generous, if that's what you mean.

Sir William. [*Dryly*] We will put it that way. [*A pause.*] At the present moment you owe, as I understand it, eleven hundred pounds.

Bill. About that.

Sir William. Mere flea-bite. [*A pause.*] I've a proposition to make.

Bill. Won't it do to-morrow, sir?

Sir William. "To-morrow" appears to be your motto in life.

Bill. Thanks!

Sir William. I'm anxious to change it to "To-day." [Bill *looks at him in silence.*] It's time you took your position seriously, instead of hanging about town, racing, and playing polo, and what not.

Bill. Go ahead!

> [*At something dangerous in his voice,* Sir William *modifies his attitude.*

Sir William. The proposition's very simple. I can't suppose anything so rational and to your advantage will appeal to you, but [*dryly*] I mention it. Marry a nice girl, settle down, and stand for the division; you can have the Dower House and fifteen hundred a year, and I'll pay your debts into the bargain. If you're elected I'll make it two thousand. Plenty of time to work up the constituency before we kick out these infernal Rads. Carpet-bagger against you; if you go hard at it in the summer, it'll be odd if you don't manage to put in your three days a week, next season.   You can take Rocketer and that four-year-old—he's well up to your weight, fully eight and a half inches of bone. You'll only want one other.   And if Miss—if your wife means to hunt——

BILL. You've chosen my wife, then?

SIR WILLIAM. [*With a quick look*] I imagine, you've some girl in your mind.

BILL. Ah!

SIR WILLIAM. Used not to be unnatural at your age.   I married your mother at twenty-eight.   Here you are, eldest son of a family that stands for something.   The more I see of the times the more I'm convinced that everybody who is anybody has got to buckle to, and save the landmarks left. Unless we're true to our caste, and prepared to work for it, the landed classes are going to go under to this infernal democratic spirit in the air.   The outlook's very serious. We're threatened in a hundred ways.   If you mean business, you'll want a wife.   When I came into the property I should have been lost without your mother.

BILL. I thought this was coming.

SIR WILLIAM. [*With a certain geniality*] My dear fellow, I don't want to put a pistol to your head.   You've had a slack rein so far.   I've never objected to your sowing a few wild oats—so long as you—er—[*Unseen by* SIR WILLIAM, BILL *makes a sudden movement.*]   Short of that—at all events, I've not inquired into your affairs.   I can only judge by the—er— pecuniary evidence you've been good enough to afford me from time to time.   I imagine you've lived like a good many young men in your position—I'm not blaming you, but there's a time for all things.

BILL. Why don't you say outright that you want me to marry Mabel Lanfarne?

SIR WILLIAM. Well, I do.   Girl's a nice one.   Good family

—got a little money—rides well. Isn't she good-looking enough for you, or what?

BILL. Quite, thanks.

SIR WILLIAM. I understood from your mother that you and she were on good terms.

BILL. Please don't drag mother into it.

SIR WILLIAM. [*With dangerous politeness*] Perhaps you'll be good enough to state your objections.

BILL. Must we go on with this?

SIR WILLIAM. I've never asked you to do anything for me before; I expect you to pay attention now. I've no wish to dragoon you into this particular marriage. If you don't care for Miss Lanfarne, marry a girl you're fond of.

BILL. I refuse.

SIR WILLIAM. In that case you know what to look out for. [*With a sudden rush of choler.*] You young . . . [*He checks himself and stands glaring at* BILL, *who glares back at him.*] This means, I suppose, that you've got some entanglement or other.

BILL. Suppose what you like, sir.

SIR WILLIAM. I warn you, if you play the blackguard——

BILL. You can't force me like young Dunning.

[*Hearing the raised voices* LADY CHESHIRE *has come back from the billiard-room.*

LADY CHESHIRE. [*Closing the door*] What is it?

SIR WILLIAM. You deliberately refuse! Go away, Dorothy.

LADY CHESHIRE. [*Resolutely*] I haven't seen Bill for two months.

SIR WILLIAM. What! [*Hesitating.*] Well—we must talk it over again.

LADY CHESHIRE. Come to the billiard-room, both of you! Bill, *do* finish those letters!

[*With a deft movement she draws* SIR WILLIAM *toward the billiard-room, and glances back at* BILL *before going out, but he has turned to the writing-table. When the*

> *door is closed,* BILL *looks into the drawing-room, then*
> *opens the door under the stairs; and backing away*
> *towards the writing-table, sits down there, and takes*
> *up a pen.* FREDA, *who has evidently been waiting,*
> *comes in and stands by the table.*

BILL. I say, this is dangerous, you know.

FREDA. Yes—but I must.

BILL. Well, then—— [*With natural recklessness.*] Aren't you going to kiss me?

> [*Without moving she looks at him with a sort of miserable*
> *inquiry.*

BILL. Do you know you haven't seen me for eight weeks?

FREDA. Quite—long enough—for you to have forgotten.

BILL. Forgotten! I don't forget people so soon.

FREDA. No?

BILL. What's the matter with you, Freda?

FREDA. [*After a long look*] It'll never be as it was.

BILL. [*Jumping up*] How d'you mean?

FREDA. I've got something for you. [*She takes a diamond ring out of her dress and holds it out to him.*] I've not worn it since Cromer.

BILL. Now, look here——

FREDA. I've had my holiday; I shan't get another in a hurry.

BILL. Freda!

FREDA. You'll be glad to be free. That fortnight's all you really loved me in.

BILL. [*Putting his hands on her arms*] I swear——

FREDA. [*Between her teeth*] Miss Lanfarne need never know about me.

BILL. So that's it! I've told you a dozen times—nothing's changed.   [FREDA *looks at him and smiles.*

BILL. Oh! very well! If you *will* make yourself miserable.

FREDA. Everybody will be pleased.

BILL. At what?

FREDA. When you marry her.

BILL. This is too bad.

FREDA. It's what always happens—even when it's not a gentleman.

BILL. That's enough!

FREDA. But I'm not like that girl down in the village. You needn't be afraid I'll say anything when—it comes. That's what I had to tell you.

BILL. *What !*

FREDA. *I* can keep a secret.

BILL. Do you mean this?   [*She bows her head.*

BILL. Good God!

FREDA. Father brought me up not to whine. Like the puppies when they hold them up by their tails. [*With a sudden break in her voice.*] Oh! Bill!

BILL. [*With his head down, seizing her hands*] Freda! [*He breaks away from her towards the fire.*] Good God!

> [*She stands looking at him, then quietly slips away by the door under the staircase. BILL turns to speak to her, and sees that she has gone. He walks up to the fireplace, and grips the mantelpiece.*

BILL. By Jove! This is——!

The curtain falls.

ACT II

The scene is LADY CHESHIRE'S *morning room, at ten o'clock on the following day. It is a pretty room, with white panelled walls, and chrysanthemums and carmine lilies in bowls. A large bow window overlooks the park under a sou'-westerly sky. A piano stands open; a fire is burning; and the morning's correspondence is scattered on a writing-table. Doors opposite each other lead to the maid's workroom, and to a corridor.* LADY CHESHIRE *is standing in the middle of the room, looking at an opera cloak, which* FREDA *is holding out.*

LADY CHESHIRE. Well, Freda, suppose you just give it up!

FREDA. I don't like to be beaten.

LADY CHESHIRE. You're not to worry over your work. And by the way, I promised your father to make you eat more.   [FREDA *smiles.*

LADY CHESHIRE. It's all very well to smile. You want bracing up. Now don't be naughty. I shall give you a tonic. And I think you had better put that cloak away.

FREDA. I'd rather have one more try, my lady.

LADY CHESHIRE. [*Sitting down at her writing-table*] Very well.

> [FREDA *goes out into her workroom, as* JACKSON *comes in from the corridor.*

JACKSON. Excuse me, my lady. There's a young woman from the village, says you wanted to see her.

LADY CHESHIRE. Rose Taylor? Ask her to come in. Oh! and, Jackson, the car for the meet, please, at half-past ten.

[JACKSON *having bowed and withdrawn,* LADY CHESHIRE
*rises with marked signs of nervousness, which she has
only just suppressed when* ROSE TAYLOR, *a stolid
country girl, comes in and stands waiting by the
door.*

LADY CHESHIRE. Well, Rose.   Do come in!

[ROSE *advances perhaps a couple of steps.*

LADY CHESHIRE. I just wondered whether you'd like to ask
my advice.   Your engagement with Dunning's broken off,
isn't it?

ROSE. Yes—but I've told him he's got to marry me.

LADY CHESHIRE. I see!   And you think that'll be the wisest
thing?

ROSE. [*Stolidly*] I don't know, my lady.   He's *got* to.

LADY CHESHIRE. I do hope you're a little fond of him
still.

ROSE. I'm *not*.   He don't deserve it.

LADY CHESHIRE. And—do you think he's quite lost his
affection for you?

ROSE. I suppose so, else he wouldn't treat me as he's done.
He's after that—that——   He didn't ought to treat me as if I
was dead.

LADY CHESHIRE. No, no—of course.   But you *will* think
it all well over, won't you?

ROSE. I've a-got nothing to think over, except what I
know of.

LADY CHESHIRE. But for you both to marry in that spirit!
You know it's for life, Rose. [*Looking into her face.*] I'm
always ready to help you.

ROSE. [*Dropping a very slight curtsey*] Thank you, my
lady, but I think he ought to marry me.   I've told him he
ought.

LADY CHESHIRE. [*Sighing*] Well, that's all I wanted to say.
It's a question of your self-respect; I can't give you any real
advice.   But just remember that if you want a friend——

D

Rose. [*With a gulp*] I'm not so 'ard, really. I only want him to do what's right by me.

Lady Cheshire. [*With a little lift of her eyebrows—gently*] Yes—yes—I see.

Rose. [*Glancing back at the door*] I don't like meeting the servants.

Lady Cheshire. Come along, I'll take you out another way.   [*As they reach the door,* Dot *comes in.*

Dot. [*With a glance at* Rose] Can we have this room for the mouldy rehearsal, Mother?

Lady Cheshire. Yes, dear, you can air it here.

[*Holding the door open for* Rose, *she follows her out. And* Dot, *with a book of " Caste " in her hand, arranges the room according to a diagram.*

Dot. Chair—chair—table—chair—Dash! Table—piano —fire—window! [*Producing a pocket comb.*] Comb for Eccles. Cradle?—Cradle—[*She viciously dumps a waste-paper basket down, and drops a foot-stool into it.*] Brat! [*Then reading from the book gloomily.*] " Enter Eccles breathless. Esther and Polly rise—Esther puts on lid of bandbox." Bandbox!

[*Searching for something to represent a bandbox, she opens the workroom door.*

Dot. Freda?   [Freda *comes in.*

Dot. I say, Freda. Anything the matter? You seem awfully down.   [Freda *does not answer.*

Dot. You haven't looked anything of a lollipop lately.

Freda. I'm quite all right, thank you, Miss Dot.

Dot. Has Mother been givin' you a tonic?

Freda. [*Smiling a little*] Not yet.

Dot. That doesn't account for it then.   [*With a sudden warm impulse.*] What *is* it, Freda?

Freda. Nothing.

Dot. [*Switching off on a different line of thought*] Are you very busy this morning?

Freda. Only this cloak for my lady.

DOT. Oh! that can wait. I may have to get you in to prompt, if I can't keep 'em straight. [*Gloomily.*] They stray so. Would you mind?

FREDA. [*Stolidly*] I shall be very glad, Miss Dot.

DOT. [*Eyeing her dubiously*] All right. Let's see—what did I want? [JOAN *has come in.*

JOAN. Look here, Dot; about the baby in this scene. I'm sure I ought to make more of it.

DOT. Romantic little beast! [*She plucks the footstool out by one ear, and holds it forth*]. Let's see you try!

JOAN. [*Recoiling*] But, Dot, what are we really going to have for the baby? I can't rehearse with that thing. Can't *you* suggest something, Freda?

FREDA. Borrow a real one, Miss Joan. There are some that don't count much.

JOAN. Freda, how horrible!

DOT. [*Dropping the footstool back into the basket*] You'll just put up with what you're given.

> [*Then as* CHRISTINE *and* MABEL LANFARNE *come in,*
> FREDA *turns abruptly and goes out.*

DOT. Buck up! Where are Bill and Harold? [*To* JOAN.] Go and find them, mouse-cat.

> [*But* BILL *and* HAROLD, *followed by* LATTER, *are already
> in the doorway. They come in, and* LATTER,
> *stumbling over the waste-paper basket, takes it up to
> improve its position.*

DOT. Drop that cradle, John! [*As he picks the footstool out of it.*] Leave the baby in! Now then! Bill, you enter there! [*She points to the workroom door, where* BILL *and* MABEL *range themselves close to the piano; while* HAROLD *goes to the window.*] John! get off the stage! Now then, " Eccles enters breathless, Esther and Polly rise." Wait a minute. I know now. [*She opens the workroom door.*] Freda, I wanted a bandbox.

HAROLD. [*Cheerfully*] I hate beginning to rehearse, you know, you feel such a fool.

Dot. [*With her bandbox—gloomily*] You'll feel more of a fool when you have begun. [*To* Bill, *who is staring into the workroom.*] Shut the door. Now.

[Bill *shuts the door.*

Latter. [*Advancing*] Look here! I want to clear up a point of psychology before we start.

Dot. Good Lord!

Latter. When I bring in the milk—ought I to bring it in seriously—as if I were accustomed—I mean, I maintain that if I'm——

Joan. Oh! John, but I don't think it's meant that you should——

Dot. Shut up! Go back, John! Blow the milk! Begin, begin, begin! Bill!

Latter. [*Turning round and again advancing*] But I think you underrate the importance of my entrance altogether.

Mabel. Oh! no, Mr. Latter.

Latter. I don't in the least want to destroy the balance of the scene, but I do want to be clear about the spirit. What is the spirit?

Dot. [*With gloom*] Rollicking!

Latter. Well, I don't think so. We shall run a great risk with this play, if we rollick.

Dot. Shall we? Now look here——!

Mabel. [*Softly to* Bill.] Mr. Cheshire!

Bill. [*Desperately*] Let's get on!

Dot. [*Waving* Latter *back*] Begin, begin! At last!

[*But* Jackson *has come in.*

Jackson. [*To* Christine] Studdenham says, M'm, if the young ladies want to see the spaniel pups, he's brought 'em round.

Joan. [*Starting up*] Oh! come on, John!

[*She flies towards the door, followed by* Latter.

Dot. [*Gesticulating with her book*] Stop! You——!

[Christine *and* Harold *also rush past.*

DOT. [*Despairingly*] First pick! [*Tearing her hair.*] Pigs!
Devils!   [*She rushes after them.*

[BILL *and* MABEL *are left alone.*

MABEL. [*Mockingly*] And don't *you* want one of the spaniel
pups?

BILL. [*Painfully reserved and sullen, and conscious of the workroom door*] Can't keep a dog in town.   You can have one, if
you like.   The breeding's all right.

MABEL. Sixth pick?

BILL. The girls 'll give you one of theirs.   They only fancy
they want 'em.

MABEL. [*Moving nearer to him, with her hands clasped behind
her*] You know, you remind me awfully of your father.
Except that you're not nearly so polite.   I don't understand
you English—lords of the soil.   The way you have of
disposing of your females. [*With a sudden change of voice.*]
What was the matter with you last night? [*Softly.*] Won't
you tell me?

BILL. Nothing to tell.

MABEL. Ah! no, Mr. Bill.

BILL. [*Almost succumbing to her voice—then sullenly*] Worried,
I suppose.

MABEL. [*Returning to her mocking*] Quite got over it?

BILL. Don't chaff me, please.

MABEL. You really are rather formidable.

BILL. Thanks.

MABEL. But, you know, I love to cross a field where
there's a bull.

BILL. Really!   Very interesting.

MABEL. The way of their only seeing one thing at a time.
[*She moves back as he advances.*] And overturning people on
the journey.

BILL. Hadn't you better be a little careful?

MABEL. And never to see the hedge until they're stuck in it.
And then straight from that hedge into the opposite one.

BILL. [*Savagely*] What makes you bait me this morning of all mornings?

MABEL. The beautiful morning! [*Suddenly.*] It must be dull for poor Freda working in there with all this fun going on?

BILL. [*Glancing at the door*] Fun you call it?

MABEL. To go back to you, now—Mr. Cheshire.

BILL. No.

MABEL. You always make me feel so Irish. Is it because you're so English, d'you think? Ah! I can see him moving his ears. Now he's pawing the ground—He's started!

BILL. Miss Lanfarne!

MABEL. [*Still backing away from him, and drawing him on with her eyes and smile*] You can't help coming after me! [*Then with a sudden change to a sort of stern gravity.*] Can you? You'll feel that when I've gone.

> [*They stand quite still, looking into each other's eyes, and* FREDA, *who has opened the door of the workroom, stares at them.*

MABEL. [*Seeing her*] Here's the stile. *Adieu, Monsieur le taureau!*

> [*She puts her hand behind her, opens the door, and slips through, leaving* BILL *to turn, following the direction of her eyes, and see* FREDA *with the cloak still in her hand.*

BILL. [*Slowly walking owards her*] I haven't slept all night.

FREDA. No?

BILL. Have you been thinking it over?

> [FREDA *gives a bitter little laugh.*

BILL. Don't! We must make a plan. I'll get you away. I won't let you suffer. I swear I won't.

FREDA. That will be clever.

BILL. I wish to Heaven my affairs weren't in such a mess.

FREDA. I shall be—all—right, thank you.

BILL. You *must* think me a blackguard. [*She shakes her head.*] Abuse me—say something! Don't look like that!

FREDA. Were you ever really fond of me?

BILL. Of course I was, I am now. Give me your hands.

[*She looks at him, then drags her hands from his, and covers her face.*

BILL. [*Clenching his fists*] Look here! I'll prove it. [*Then as she suddenly flings her arms round his neck and clings to him.*] There, there!

[*There is a click of a door handle. They start away from each other, and see* LADY CHESHIRE *regarding them.*

LADY CHESHIRE. [*Without irony*] I beg your pardon.

[*She makes as if to withdraw from an unwarranted intrusion, but suddenly turning, stands, with lips pressed together, waiting.*

LADY CHESHIRE. Yes?

[FREDA *has muffled her face. But* BILL *turns and confronts his mother.*

BILL. Don't say anything against her!

LADY CHESHIRE. [*Tries to speak to him and fails—then to* FREDA] Please—go!

BILL. [*Taking* FREDA'S *arm*] No.

[LADY CHESHIRE, *after a moment's hesitation, herself moves towards the door.*

BILL. Stop, mother!

LADY CHESHIRE. I think perhaps not.

BILL. [*Looking at* FREDA, *who is cowering as though from a blow*] It's a d—d shame!

LADY CHESHIRE. It is.

BILL. [*With sudden resolution*] It's not as you think. I'm engaged to be married to her.

[FREDA *gives him a wild stare, and turns away.*

LADY CHESHIRE. [*Looking from one to the other*] I—don't—think—I—quite—understand.

BILL. [*With the brutality of his mortification*] What I said was plain enough.

LADY CHESHIRE. Bill!

BILL. I tell you I am going to marry her.

LADY CHESHIRE. [*To* FREDA] Is that true?

> [FREDA *gulps and remains silent.*

BILL. If you want to say anything, say it to *me*, mother.

LADY CHESHIRE. [*Gripping the edge of a little table*] Give me a chair, please.   [BILL *gives her a chair.*

LADY CHESHIRE. [*To* FREDA] Please sit down too.

> [FREDA *sits on the piano stool, still turning her face away.*

LADY CHESHIRE. [*Fixing her eyes on* FREDA] Now!

BILL. I fell in love with her.   And she with me.

LADY CHESHIRE. When!

BILL. In the summer.

LADY CHESHIRE. Ah!

BILL. It wasn't her fault.

LADY CHESHIRE. No?

BILL. [*With a sort of menace*] Mother!

LADY CHESHIRE. Forgive me, I am not quite used to the idea.   You say that you—are engaged?

BILL. Yes.

LADY CHESHIRE. The reasons against such an engagement have occurred to you, I suppose? [*With a sudden change of tone.*] Bill! what does it mean?

BILL. If you think she's trapped me into this——

LADY CHESHIRE. I do not.   Neither do I think she has been trapped.   I think nothing.   I understand nothing.

BILL. [*Grimly*] Good!

LADY CHESHIRE. How long has this—engagement lasted?

BILL. [*After a silence*] Two months.

LADY CHESHIRE. [*Suddenly*] This is—this is quite impossible.

BILL. You'll find it isn't.

LADY CHESHIRE. It's simple misery.

BILL. [*Pointing to the workroom*] Go and wait in there, Freda.

LADY CHESHIRE. [*Quickly*] And are you still in love with her?

> [FREDA, *moving towards the workroom, smothers a sob.*

BILL. Of course I am.

[FREDA *has gone, and as she goes,* LADY CHESHIRE *rises suddenly, forced by the intense feeling she has been keeping in hand.*

LADY CHESHIRE. Bill! Oh, Bill! What does it all mean? [BILL, *looking from side to side, only shrugs his shoulders.*] You are *not* in love with her now. It's no good telling me you are.

BILL. I am.

LADY CHESHIRE. That's not exactly how you would speak if you were.

BILL. She's in love with me.

LADY CHESHIRE. [*Bitterly*] I suppose so.

BILL. I mean to see that nobody runs her down.

LADY CHESHIRE. [*With difficulty*] Bill! Am I a hard, or mean woman?

BILL. Mother!

LADY CHESHIRE. It's all your life—and—your father's—and —all of us. I want to understand—I must understand. Have you realized what an awful thing this would be for us all? It's quite impossible that it should go on.

BILL. I'm always in hot water with the Governor, as it is. She and I'll take good care not to be in the way.

LADY CHESHIRE. Tell me everything!

BILL. I have.

LADY CHESHIRE. I'm your mother, Bill.

BILL. What's the good of these questions?

LADY CHESHIRE. You won't give her away—I see!

BILL. I've told you all there is to tell. We're engaged, we shall be married quietly, and—and—go to Canada.

LADY CHESHIRE. If there weren't more than that to tell you'd be in love with her now.

BILL. I've told you that I am.

LADY CHESHIRE. You are *not*. [*Almost fiercely.*] I know—I know there's more behind.

BILL. There—is—nothing.

LADY CHESHIRE. [*Baffled, but unconvinced*] Do you mean that your love for her has been just what it might have been for a lady?

BILL. [*Bitterly*] Why not?

LADY CHESHIRE. [*With painful irony*] It is not so as a rule.

BILL. Up to now I've never heard you or the girls say a word against Freda. This isn't the moment to begin, please.

LADY CHESHIRE. [*Solemnly*] All such marriages end in wretchedness. You haven't a taste or tradition in common. You don't know what marriage is. Day after day, year after year. It's no use being sentimental—for people brought up as we are, to have different manners is worse than to have different souls. Besides, it's poverty. Your father will never forgive you, and I've practically nothing. What can you do? You have no profession. How are you going to stand it; with a woman who——? It's the little things.

BILL. I know all that, thanks.

LADY CHESHIRE. Nobody does till they've been through it. Marriage is hard enough when people are of the same class. [*With a sudden movement towards him.*] Oh! my dear—before it's too late!

BILL. [*After a struggle*] It's no good.

LADY CHESHIRE. It's not fair to her. It *can* only end in her misery.

BILL. Leave that to me, please.

LADY CHESHIRE. [*With an almost angry vehemence*] Only the very finest can do such things. And you—don't even know what trouble's like.

BILL. Drop it, please, Mother.

LADY CHESHIRE. Bill, on your word of honour, are you acting of your own free will?

BILL. [*Breaking away from her*] I can't stand any more.

[*He goes out into the workroom.*

LADY CHESHIRE. What in God's name shall I do?

[*In her distress she stands quite still, then goes to the work-room door, and opens it.*

LADY CHESHIRE. Come in here, please, Freda.

[*After a second's pause,* FREDA, *white and trembling, appears in the doorway, followed by* BILL.

LADY CHESHIRE. No, Bill.   I want to speak to her alone.

[BILL *does not move.*

LADY CHESHIRE. [*Icily*] I must ask you to leave us.

[BILL *hesitates ; then shrugging his shoulders, he touches* FREDA's *arms, and goes back into the workroom, closing the door.   There is silence.*

LADY CHESHIRE. How did it come about?

FREDA. I don't know, my lady.

LADY CHESHIRE. For heaven's sake, child, don't call me that again, whatever happens. [*She walks to the window, and speaks from there.*] I know well enough how love comes. I don't blame you. Don't cry. But, you see, it's my eldest son. [FREDA *puts her hand to her breast.*] Yes, I know. Women always get the worst of these things. That's natural. But it's not only you—is it? Does anyone guess?

FREDA. No.

LADY CHESHIRE. Not even your father? [FREDA *shakes her head.*] There's nothing more dreadful than for a woman to hang like a stone round a man's neck.   How far has it gone? Tell me !

FREDA. I can't !

LADY CHESHIRE. Come !

FREDA. I—won't.

LADY CHESHIRE. [*Smiling painfully*] Won't give him away? Both of you the same.   What's the use of that with me? Look at me ! Wasn't he with you when you went for your holiday this summer?

FREDA. He's—always—behaved—like—a—gentleman.

LADY CHESHIRE. Like a *man*—you mean!

FREDA. It hasn't been his fault! I love him so.

[LADY CHESHIRE *turns abruptly, and begins to walk up and down the room.   Then stopping, she looks intently at* FREDA.

LADY CHESHIRE. I don't know what to say to you. It's simple madness! It can't, and shan't go on.

FREDA. [*Sullenly*] I know I'm not his equal, but I am—somebody.

LADY CHESHIRE. [*Answering this first assertion of rights with a sudden steeliness*] Does he love you *now*?

FREDA. That's not fair—it's not fair.

LADY CHESHIRE. If men are like gunpowder, Freda, women are not. If you've lost him it's been your own fault.

FREDA. But he *does* love me, he must. It's only four months.

LADY CHESHIRE. [*Looking down, and speaking rapidly*] Listen to me. I love my son, but I know him—I know all his kind of man. I've lived with one for thirty years. I know the way their senses work. When they want a thing they must have it, and then—they're sorry.

FREDA. [*Sullenly*] He's *not* sorry.

LADY CHESHIRE. Is his love big enough to carry you both over everything? . . . You know it isn't.

FREDA. If I were a lady, you wouldn't talk like that.

LADY CHESHIRE. If you were a lady there'd be no trouble before either of you. You'll make him hate you.

FREDA. I won't believe it. I could make him happy—out there.

LADY CHESHIRE. I don't want to be so odious as to say all the things you must know. I only ask you to try and put yourself in our position.

FREDA. Ah, yes!

LADY CHESHIRE. You ought to know me better than to think I'm purely selfish.

FREDA. Would you like to put yourself in my position?

[*She throws up her head.*

LADY CHESHIRE. What!

FREDA. Yes. Just like Rose.

LADY CHESHIRE. [*In a low, horror-stricken voice*] Oh!

[*There is a dead silence; then going swiftly up to her, she looks straight into* FREDA'S *eyes.*

FREDA. [*Meeting her gaze*] Oh! yes—it's the truth. [*Then to* BILL, *who has come in from the workroom, she gasps out.*] I never meant to tell.

BILL. Well, are you satisfied?

LADY CHESHIRE. [*Below her breath*] This is terrible!

BILL. The Governor had better know.

LADY CHESHIRE. Oh! no; not yet!

BILL. Waiting won't cure it!

[*The door from the corridor is thrown open;* CHRISTINE *and* DOT *run in with their copies of the play in their hands; seeing that something is wrong, they stand still. After a look at his mother,* BILL *turns abruptly, and goes back into the workroom.* LADY CHESHIRE *moves towards the window.*

JOAN. [*Following her sisters*] The car's round. What's the matter?

DOT. Shut up!

[SIR WILLIAM'S *voice is heard from the corridor calling "Dorothy!" As* LADY CHESHIRE, *passing her handkerchief over her face, turns round, he enters. He is in full hunting dress; well-weathered pink, buckskins, and mahogany tops.*

SIR WILLIAM. Just off, my dear. [*To his daughters, genially.*] Rehearsin'? What! [*He goes up to* FREDA, *holding out his gloved right hand.*] Button that for me, Freda, would you? It's a bit stiff!

[FREDA *buttons the glove:* LADY CHESHIRE *and the girls watching in hypnotic silence.*

SIR WILLIAM. Thank you! "Balmy as May"; scent ought to be first-rate. [*To* LADY CHESHIRE.] Good-bye, my dear! Sampson's Gorse—best day of the whole year. [*He pats* JOAN *on the shoulder.*] Wish you were comin' out, Joan.

> [*He goes out, leaving the door open, and as his footsteps and the chink of his spurs die away,* FREDA *turns and rushes into the workroom.*

CHRISTINE. Mother! What——?

> [*But* LADY CHESHIRE *waves the question aside, passes her daughter, and goes out into the corridor. The sound of a motor-car is heard.*

JOAN. [*Running to the window*] They've started!—Chris! What is it? Dot?

DOT. Bill, and her!

JOAN. But *what*?

DOT. [*Gloomily*] Heaven knows! Go away, you're not fit for this.

JOAN. [*Aghast*] I am fit.

DOT. I think not.

JOAN. Chris?

CHRISTINE. [*In a hard voice*] Mother ought to have told us.

JOAN. It can't be very awful. Freda's so *good*.

DOT. Call yourself in love, you—milky kitten!

CHRISTINE. It's horrible, not knowing anything! I *wish* Ronny hadn't gone.

JOAN. Shall I fetch John?

DOT. John!

CHRISTINE. Perhaps Harold knows.

JOAN. He went out with Studdenham.

DOT. It's always like this, women kept in blinkers. Rose-leaves and humbug! That awful old man!

JOAN. Dot!

CHRISTINE. Don't talk of father like that!

DOT. Well, he is! And Bill will be just like him at fifty!

Heaven help Freda, whatever she's done! I'd sooner be a private in a German regiment than a woman.

JOAN. Dot, you're awful!

DOT. You—mouse-hearted—linnet!

CHRISTINE. Don't talk that nonsense about women!

DOT. You're married and out of it; and Ronny's not one of these terrific John Bulls. [*To* JOAN, *who has opened the door.*] Looking for John? No good, my dear; lath and plaster.

JOAN. [*From the door, in a frightened whisper*] Here's Mabel!

DOT. Heavens, and the waters under the earth!

CHRISTINE. If we only *knew* !

> [*As* MABEL *comes in, the three girls are silent, with their eyes fixed on their books.*

MABEL. The silent company.

DOT. [*Looking straight at her*] We're chucking it for to-day.

MABEL. What's the matter.

CHRISTINE. Oh! nothing.

DOT. Something's happened.

MABEL. Really! I *am* sorry. [*Hesitating*]. Is it bad enough for me to go?

CHRISTINE. Oh! no, Mabel!

DOT. [*Sardonically*] I should think very likely.

> [*While she is looking from face to face,* BILL *comes in from the workroom. He starts to walk across the room, but stops, and looks stolidly at the four girls.*

BILL. Exactly! Fact of the matter is, Miss Lanfarne, I'm engaged to my mother's maid.

> [*No one moves or speaks. Suddenly* MABEL LANFARNE *goes towards him, holding out her hand.* BILL *does not take her hand, but bows. Then after a swift glance at the girls' faces* MABEL *goes out into the corridor, and the three girls are left staring at their brother.*

BILL. [*Coolly*] Thought you might like to know.

[*He, too, goes out into the corridor.*

CHRISTINE. Great heavens!

JOAN. How *awful*!

CHRISTINE. I never thought of anything as bad as that.

JOAN. Oh! Chris! Something must be done!

DOT. [*Suddenly to herself*] Ha! When Father went up to have his glove buttoned!

[*There is a sound,* JACKSON *has come in from the corridor.*

JACKSON. [*To* DOT] If you please, Miss, Studdenham's brought up the other two pups. He's just outside. Will you kindly take a look at them, he says?   [*There is silence.*

DOT. [*Suddenly*] We can't.

CHRISTINE. Not just now, Jackson.

JACKSON. Is Studdenham and the pups to wait, M'm?

[DOT *shakes her head violently. But* STUDDENHAM *is seen already standing in the doorway, with a spaniel puppy in either side-pocket. He comes in, and* JACKSON *stands waiting behind him.*

STUDDENHAM. This fellow's the best, Miss Dot. [*He protrudes the right-hand pocket.*] I was keeping him for my girl—a proper breedy one—takes after his father.

[*The girls stare at him in silence.*

DOT. [*Hastily*] Thanks, Studdenham, I see.

STUDDENHAM. I won't take 'em out in here. They're rather bold yet.

CHRISTINE. [*Desperately*] No, no, of course.

STUDDENHAM. Then you think you'd like him, Miss Dot? The other's got a white chest; she's a lady.

[*He protrudes the left-hand pocket.*

DOT. Oh, yes! Studdenham; thanks, thanks awfully.

STUDDENHAM. Wonderful faithful creatures; follow you like a woman. You can't shake 'em off anyhow. [*He protrudes the right-hand pocket.*] My girl, she'd set her heart on *him*, but she'll just have to do without.

DOT. [*As though galvanized*] Oh! no, I can't take it away from *her*.

STUDDENHAM. Bless you, she won't mind! That's settled, then. [*He turns to the door. To the puppy.*] Ah! would you! Tryin' to wriggle out of it! Regular young limb!

[*He goes out, followed by* JACKSON.

CHRISTINE. How ghastly!

DOT. [*Suddenly catching sight of the book in her hand*] Caste !

[*She gives vent to a short sharp laugh.*

The curtain falls.

ACT III

It is five o'clock of the same day.   The scene is the smoking-room, with walls of Leander red, covered by old steeplechase and and hunting prints.   Armchairs encircle a high-fendered hearth, in which a fire is burning.   The curtains are not yet drawn across mullioned windows;   but electric light is burning. There are two doors, leading, the one to the billiard-room, the other to a corridor.   BILL is pacing up and down; HAROLD, at the fireplace, stands looking at him with commiseration.

BILL. What's the time?

HAROLD. Nearly five.   They won't be in yet, if that's any consolation.   Always a good meet—[*softly*] as the tiger said when he ate the man.

BILL. By Jove !   You're the only person I can stand within a mile of me, Harold.

HAROLD. Old boy ! Do you seriously think you're going to make it any better by marrying her?

[BILL *shrugs his shoulders, still pacing the room.*

HAROLD. Well, then?

BILL. Look here ! I'm not the sort that finds it easy to say things.

HAROLD. No, old man.

BILL. But I've got a kind of self-respect though you wouldn't think it !

HAROLD. My dear old chap !

BILL. This is about as low-down a thing as one could have done, I suppose—one's own mother's maid; we've known her since she was so high. I see it now that—I've got over the attack.

HAROLD. But, heavens! if you're no longer keen on her, Bill! Do apply your reason, old boy.

[*There is silence ; while* BILL *again paces up and down.*

BILL. If you think I care two straws about the morality of the thing——

HAROLD. Oh! my dear old man! Of course not!

BILL. It's simply that I shall feel such a d—d skunk, if I leave her in the lurch, with everybody knowing. Try it yourself; you'd soon see!

HAROLD. Poor old chap!

BILL. It's not as if she'd tried to force me into it. And she's a soft little thing. Why I ever made such a sickening ass of myself, I can't think. I never meant——

HAROLD. No, I know! But, don't do anything rash, Bill; keep your head, old man!

BILL. I don't see what loss I should be, if I did clear out of the country. [*The sound of cannoning billiard balls is heard.*] Who's that knocking the balls about?

HAROLD. John, I expect. [*The sound ceases.*

BILL. He's coming in here. Can't stand that!

[*As* LATTER *appears from the billiard-room, he goes hurriedly out.*

LATTER. Was that Bill?

HAROLD. Yes.

LATTER. Well?

HAROLD. [*Pacing up and down in his turn*] Cat on hot bricks is nothing to him. This is the sort of thing you read of in books, John! What price your argument with Ronny now? Well, it's not too late for *you* luckily.

LATTER. What do you mean?

HAROLD. You needn't connect yourself with this eccentric family.

LATTER. I'm not a bounder Harold.

HAROLD. Good!

LATTER. It's terrible for your sisters.

HAROLD. Deuced lucky we haven't a lot of people staying here! Poor mother! John, I feel awfully bad about this. If something isn't done, pretty mess I shall be in.

LATTER. How?

HAROLD. There's no entail. If the Governor cuts Bill off, it'll all come to me.

LATTER. Oh!

HAROLD. Poor old Bill! I say, the play! Nemesis What? Moral! Caste don't matter. Got us fairly on the hop.

LATTER. It's too bad of Bill. It really is. He's behaved disgracefully.

HAROLD. [*Warmly*] Well! There are thousands of fellows who'd never dream of sticking to the girl, considering what it means.

LATTER. Perfectly disgusting!

HAROLD. Hang you, John! Haven't you any human sympathy? Don't you know how these things come about? It's like a spark in a straw-yard.

LATTER. One doesn't take lighted pipes into straw-yards unless one's an idiot, or worse.

HAROLD. H'm! [*With a grin.*] *You're* not allowed tobacco. In the good old days no one would have thought anything of this. My great-grandfather——

LATTER. Spare me your great-grandfather.

HAROLD. I could tell you of at least a dozen men I know who've been through this same business, and got off scot-free; and now because Bill's going to play the game, it'll smash him up.

LATTER. Why didn't he play the game at the beginning?

HAROLD. I can't stand your sort, John. When a thing like this happens, all you can do is to cry out: Why didn't he——? Why didn't she——? What's to be *done*—that's the point!

LATTER. Of course he'll have to——

HAROLD. Ha!

LATTER. What do you mean by—that?

HAROLD. Look here, John! You feel in your bones that a marriage'll be hopeless, just as I do, knowing Bill and the girl and everything! Now don't you?

LATTER. The whole thing is—is most unfortunate.

HAROLD. By Jove! I should think it was!

[*As he speaks* CHRISTINE *and* KEITH *come in from the billiard-room. He is still in splashed hunting clothes, and looks exceptionally weathered, thin-lipped, reticent. He lights a cigarette and sinks into an armchair. Behind them* DOT *and* JOAN *have come stealing in.*

CHRISTINE. I've told Ronny.

JOAN. This waiting for father to be told is awful.

HAROLD. [*To* KEITH] Where did you leave the old man?

KEITH. Clackenham. He'll be home in ten minutes.

DOT. Mabel's going. [*They all stir, as if at fresh consciousness of discomfiture.*] She walked into Gracely, and sent herself a telegram.

HAROLD. Phew!

DOT. And we shall say good-bye as if nothing had happened!

HAROLD. It's up to you, Ronny.

[KEITH, *looking at* JOAN, *slowly emits smoke; and* LATTER *passing his arm through* JOAN'S, *draws her away with him into the billiard-room.*

KEITH. Dot?

DOT. *I'm* not a squeamy squirrel.

KEITH. Anybody seen the girl since?

DOT. Yes.

HAROLD. Well?

DOT. She's just sitting there.

CHRISTINE. [*In a hard voice*] As we're all doing.

DOT. She's so soft, that's what's so horrible. If one could only feel——!

KEITH. She's got to face the music like the rest of us.

DOT. Music! Squeaks! Ugh! The whole thing's like a concertina, and some one jigging it!

[*They all turn as the door opens, and a* FOOTMAN *enters with a tray of whisky, gin, lemons, and soda water. In dead silence the* FOOTMAN *puts the tray down.*

HAROLD. [*Forcing his voice*] Did you get a run, Ronny? [*As* KEITH *nods.*] What point?

KEITH. Eight mile.

FOOTMAN. Will you take tea, sir?

KEITH. No, thanks, Charles!

[*In dead silence again the* FOOTMAN *goes out, and they all look after him.*

HAROLD. [*Below his breath*] Good Gad! That's a queeze of it!

KEITH. What's our line of country to be?

CHRISTINE. All depends on father.

KEITH. Sir William's between the devil and the deep sea, as it strikes me.

CHRISTINE. He'll simply forbid it utterly, of course.

KEITH. H'm! Hard case! Man who reads family prayers, and lessons on Sunday forbids son to——

CHRISTINE. Ronny!

KEITH. Great Scot! I'm not saying Bill ought to marry her. She's got to stand the racket. But your Dad will have a tough job to take up that position.

DOT. Awfully funny!

CHRISTINE. What on earth d'you mean, Dot?

DOT. Morality in one eye, and your title in the other!

CHRISTINE. Rubbish!

HAROLD. You're all reckoning without your Bill.

KEITH. Ye-es. Sir William can cut him off; no mortal power can help the title going down, if Bill chooses to be uch a——   [*He draws in his breath with a sharp hiss.*

HAROLD. I won't take what Bill ought to have; nor would any of you girls, I should think——

CHRISTINE and DOT. Of course not!

KEITH. [*Patting his wife's arm*] Hardly the point, is it?

DOT. If it wasn't for mother! Freda's just as much of a lady as most girls. Why shouldn't he marry her, and go to Canada? It's what he's really fit for.

HAROLD. Steady on, Dot!

DOT. Well, imagine him in Parliament! That's what he'll come to, if he stays here—jolly for the country!

CHRISTINE. Don't be cynical! We must find a way of stopping Bill.

DOT. *Me* cynical!

CHRISTINE. Let's go and beg him, Ronny!

KEITH. No earthly! The only hope is in the girl.

DOT. She hasn't the stuff in her!

HAROLD. I say! What price young Dunning! Right about face! Poor old Dad!

CHRISTINE. It's past joking, Harold!

DOT. [*Gloomily*] Old Studdenham's better than most relations by marriage!

KEITH. Thanks!

CHRISTINE. It's ridiculous—monstrous! It's fantastic!

HAROLD. [*Holding up his hand*] There's his horse going round. He's in!

> [*They turn from listening to the sound, to see* LADY CHESHIRE *coming from the billiard-room. She is very pale. They all rise and* DOT *puts an arm round her; while* KEITH *pushes forward his chair.* JOAN *and* LATTER *too have come stealing back.*

LADY CHESHIRE. Thank you, Ronny!   [*She sits down.*

DOT. Mother, you're shivering! Shall I get you a fur?

LADY CHESHIRE. No, thanks, dear!

DOT. [*In a low voice*] Play up, mother darling!

LADY CHESHIRE. [*Straightening herself*] What sort of a run, Ronny?

KEITH. Quite fair, M'm.   Brazier's to Caffyn's Dyke, good straight line.

LADY CHESHIRE. And the young horse?

KEITH. Carries his ears in your mouth a bit, that's all. [*Putting his hand on her shoulder.*] Cheer up, Mem-Sahib!

CHRISTINE. Mother, *must* anything be said to father? Ronny thinks it all depends on *her*.   Can't you use your influence?   [LADY CHESHIRE *shakes her head.*

CHRISTINE. But, mother, it's desperate.

DOT. Shut up, Chris!   Of course mother can't.   We simply couldn't *beg* her to let us off!

CHRISTINE. There must be *some* way.   What do you think in your heart, mother?

DOT. Leave mother alone!

CHRISTINE. It must be faced, now or never.

DOT. [*In a low voice*] Haven't you any self-respect?

CHRISTINE. We shall be the laughing-stock of the whole county.   Oh! mother, do speak to her!   You know it'll be misery for both of them.   [LADY CHESHIRE *bows her head.*] Well, then?   [LADY CHESHIRE *shakes her head.*

CHRISTINE. Not even for Bill's sake?

DOT. Chris!

CHRISTINE. Well, for heaven's sake, speak to Bill again, mother!   We ought all to go on our knees to him.

LADY CHESHIRE. He's with your father now.

HAROLD. Poor old Bill!

CHRISTINE. [*Passionately*] He didn't think of *us*!   That wretched girl!

LADY CHESHIRE. Chris!

CHRISTINE. There are limits.

LADY CHESHIRE. Not to self-control.

CHRISTINE. No, mother!   I can't—I never shall—Something must be done!   You know what Bill is.   He rushes his fences so, when he gets his head down. Oh! do try! It's only fair to her, and all of us!

LADY CHESHIRE. [*Painfully*] There are things one can't do.

CHRISTINE. But it's Bill! I know you can make her give him up, if you'll only say all you can. And, after all, what's coming won't affect her as if she'd been a lady. Only *you* can do it, mother. Do back me up, all of you! It's the only way!

> [*Hypnotized by their private longing for what* CHRISTINE *has been urging, they have all fixed their eyes on* LADY CHESHIRE, *who looks from face to face, and moves her hands as if in physical pain.*

CHRISTINE. [*Softly*] Mother!

> [LADY CHESHIRE *suddenly rises, looking towards the billiard-room door, listening. They all follow her eyes. She sits down again, passing her hand over her lips, as* SIR WILLIAM *enters. His hunting clothes are splashed; his face very grim and set. He walks to the fire without a glance at anyone, and stands looking down into it. Very quietly, everyone but* LADY CHESHIRE *steals away.*

LADY CHESHIRE. What have you done?

SIR WILLIAM. *You* there!

LADY CHESHIRE. Don't keep me in suspense!

SIR WILLIAM. The fool! My God! Dorothy! I didn't think I had a blackguard for a son, who was a fool into the bargain.

LADY CHESHIRE. [*Rising*] If he were a blackguard he would not be what you call a fool.

SIR WILLIAM. [*After staring angrily, makes her a slight bow*] Very well!

LADY CHESHIRE. [*In a low voice*] Bill, don't be harsh. It's all too terrible.

SIR WILLIAM. Sit down, my dear.

> [*She resumes her seat, and he turns back to the fire.*

Sir William. In all my life I've never been face to face with a thing like this. [*Gripping the mantelpiece so hard that his hands and arms are seen shaking.*] You ask me to be calm. I am trying to be. Be good enough in turn not to take his part against me.

Lady Cheshire. Bill!

Sir William. I am trying to think. I understand that you've known this—piece of news since this morning. I've known it ten minutes. Give me a little time, please. [*Then, after a silence.*] Where's the girl?

Lady Cheshire. In the workroom.

Sir William. [*Raising his clenched fist*] What in God's name is he about?

Lady Cheshire. What have you said to him?

Sir William. Nothing—by a miracle. [*He breaks away from the fire and walks up and down.*] My family goes back to the thirteenth century. Nowadays they laugh at that! I don't! Nowadays they laugh at everything—they even laugh at the word lady—I married *you*, and I don't. . . . Married his mother's maid! By George! Dorothy! I don't know what we've done to deserve this; it's a death blow! I'm not prepared to sit down and wait for it. By Gad! I am not. [*With sudden fierceness.*] There are plenty in these days who'll be glad enough for this to happen; plenty of these d——d Socialists and Radicals, who'll laugh their souls out over what they haven't the bowels to see's a—tragedy. I say it *would* be a tragedy; for you, and me, and all of us. You and I were brought up, and we've brought the children up, with certain beliefs, and wants, and habits. A man's past—his traditions—he can't get rid of them. They're—they're himself! [*Suddenly.*] It shan't go on.

Lady Cheshire. What's to prevent it?

Sir William. I utterly forbid this piece of madness. I'll stop it.

Lady Cheshire. But the thing we can't stop.

SIR WILLIAM. Provision must be made.

LADY CHESHIRE. The unwritten law!

SIR WILLIAM. What! [*Suddenly perceiving what she is alluding to.*] You're thinking of young—young—— [*Shortly.*] I don't see the connection.

LADY CHESHIRE. What's so awful, is that the boy's trying to do what's loyal—and we—his father and mother——!

SIR WILLIAM. I'm not going to see my eldest son ruin his life. I must think this out.

LADY CHESHIRE. [*Beneath her breath*] I've tried that—it doesn't help.

SIR WILLIAM. This girl, who was born on the estate, had the run of the house—brought up with money earned from me—nothing but kindness from all of us; she's broken the common rules of gratitude and decency—she lured him on, I haven't a doubt!

LADY CHESHIRE. [*To herself*] In a way, I suppose.

SIR WILLIAM. What! It's ruin. We've always been here. Who the deuce are we if we leave this place? D'you think we could stay? Go out and meet everybody just as if nothing had happened? Good-bye to any prestige, political, social, or anything! This is the sort of business nothing can get over. I've seen it before. As to that other matter—it's soon forgotten—constantly happening—Why, my own grand-father——!

LADY CHESHIRE. Does he help?

SIR WILLIAM. [*Stares before him in silence—suddenly*] You must go to the girl. She's soft. She'll never hold out against you.

LADY CHESHIRE. I did before I knew what was in front of her—I said all I could. I can't go again now. How can I, Bill?

SIR WILLIAM. What *are* you going to do, then—fold your hands? [*Then as* LADY CHESHIRE *makes a movement of distress.*] If he marries her, I've done with him. As far as I'm concerned he'll cease to exist.   The title—I can't help.   My God!   Does that meet your wishes?

LADY CHESHIRE. [*With sudden fire*] You've no right to put such an alternative to me.   I'd give ten years of my life to prevent this marriage.   I'll go to Bill.   I'll beg him on my knees.

SIR WILLIAM. Then why can't you go to the girl?   She deserves no consideration.   It's not a question of morality.   Morality be d——d!

LADY CHESHIRE. But not self-respect.

SIR WILLIAM. What!   You're his mother!

LADY CHESHIRE. I have been to her;   I've tried;   I [*putting her hand to her throat*] couldn't get it out.

SIR WILLIAM. [*Staring at her*] You won't?

LADY CHESHIRE. I can't, Bill.   It seems so—caddish, so mean.

SIR WILLIAM. In the whole course of our married life, Dorothy, I've never known you set yourself up against me. I resent this, I warn you—I resent it.   Send the girl to me.

> [*With a look back at him,* LADY CHESHIRE *goes out into the corridor.*

SIR WILLIAM. This is a nice end to my day!

> [*He takes a small china cup from off the mantelpiece; it breaks with the pressure of his hand, and falls into the fireplace.   While he stands looking at it blankly, there is a knock.*

SIR WILLIAM. Come in!   [FREDA *enters from the corridor.*

SIR WILLIAM. I've asked you to be good enough to come, in order that— [*pointing to chair*] You may sit down.

> [*But though she advances two or three steps, she does not sit down.*

SIR WILLIAM. This is a sad business.

FREDA. [*Below her breath*] Yes, Sir William.

SIR WILLIAM. [*Becoming conscious of the depths of feeling before him*] I—er—are you attached to my son?

FREDA. [*In a whisper*] Yes.

SIR WILLIAM. It's very painful to me to have to do this.
          [*He turns away from her and speaks to the fire.*]
I sent for you—to—ask— [*quickly*] How old are you?

FREDA. Twenty-two.

SIR WILLIAM. [*More resolutely*] Do you expect me to—
sanction such a mad idea as a marriage?

FREDA. I don't expect anything.

SIR WILLIAM. You know—you haven't earned the right to
be considered.

FREDA. Not yet!

SIR WILLIAM. What! That oughtn't to help you!
On the contrary. Now brace yourself up, and listen to
me!

          [*She stands waiting to hear her sentence. SIR WILLIAM
          looks at her; and his glance gradually wavers.*

SIR WILLIAM. I've not a word to say for my son. He's
behaved like a scamp.

FREDA. Oh! no!

SIR WILLIAM. [*With a silencing gesture*] At the same time—
What made you forget yourself? You've no excuse, you
know.

FREDA. No.

SIR WILLIAM. You'll deserve all you'll get. Confound it!
To expect me to— It's intolerable! Do you know where
my son is?

FREDA. [*Faintly*] I think he's in the billiard-room with my
lady.

SIR WILLIAM. [*With renewed resolution*] I wanted to—to
put it to you—as a—as a—what! [*Seeing her stand so
absolutely motionless, looking at him, he turns abruptly, and opens
the billiard-room door.*] I'll speak to him first. Come in here,
please! [*To FREDA.*] Go in, and wait!

          [LADY CHESHIRE *and* BILL *come in, and* FREDA *passing
          him, goes into the billiard-room to wait.*

SIR WILLIAM. [*Speaking with a pause between each sentence*] Your mother and I have spoken of this—calamity. I imagine that even you have some dim perception of the monstrous nature of it. I must tell you this: If you do this mad thing, you fend for yourself. You'll receive nothing from me now or hereafter. I consider that only due to the position our family has always held here. Your brother will take your place. We shall get on as best we can without you. [*There is a dead silence, till he adds sharply.*] Well!

BILL. I shall marry her.

LADY CHESHIRE. Oh! Bill! Without love—without anything!

BILL. All right, mother! [*To* SIR WILLIAM.] You've mistaken your man, sir. Because I'm a rotter in one way, I'm not necessarily a rotter in all. You put the butt end of the pistol to Dunning's head yesterday, you put the other end to mine to-day. Well! [*He turns round to go out.*] Let the d——d thing off!

LADY CHESHIRE. Bill!

BILL. [*Turning to her*] I'm not going to leave her in the lurch.

SIR WILLIAM. Do me the justice to admit that I have not attempted to persuade you to.

BILL. No! you've chucked me out. I don't see what else you could have done under the circumstances. It's quite all right. But if you wanted me to throw her over, father, you went the wrong way to work, that's all; neither you nor I are very good at seeing consequences.

SIR WILLIAM. Do you realize your position?

BILL. [*Grimly*] I've a fair notion of it.

SIR WILLIAM. [*With a sudden outburst*] You have none—not the faintest, brought up as you've been.

BILL. I didn't bring myself up.

SIR WILLIAM. [*With a movement of uncontrolled anger, to which his son responds*] You—ungrateful young dog!

LADY CHESHIRE. How can you—both?

[*They drop their eyes, and stand silent.*

SIR WILLIAM. [*With grimly suppressed emotion*] I am speaking under the stress of very great pain—some consideration is due to me. This is a disaster which I never expected to have to face. It is a matter which I naturally can never hope to forget. I shall carry this down to my death. We shall all of us do that. I have had the misfortune all my life to believe in our position here—to believe that we counted for something—that the country wanted us. I have tried to do my duty by that position. I find in one moment that it is gone—smoke—gone. My philosophy is not equal to that. To countenance this marriage would be unnatural.

BILL. I know. I'm sorry. I've got her into this—I don't see any other way out. It's a bad business for me, father, as well as for you——

[*He stops, seeing that* JACKSON *has come in, and is standing there waiting.*

JACKSON. Will you speak to Studdenham, Sir William? It's about young Dunning.

[*After a moment of dead silence,* SIR WILLIAM *nods, and the butler withdraws.*

BILL. [*Stolidly*] He'd better be told.

SIR WILLIAM. He shall be.

[STUDDENHAM *enters, and touches his forehead to them all with a comprehensive gesture.*

STUDDENHAM. Good evenin', my lady! Evenin', Sir William! Glad to be able to tell you, the young man's to do the proper thing. Asked me to let you know, Sir William. Banns'll be up next Sunday. [*Struck by the silence, he looks round at all three in turn, and suddenly seeing that* LADY CHESHIRE *is shivering.*] Beg pardon, my lady, you're shakin' like a leaf!

BILL. [*Blurting it out*] I've a painful piece of news for you, Studdenham; I'm engaged to your daughter. We're to be married at once.

STUDDENHAM. I—don't—understand you—sir.

BILL. The fact is, I've behaved badly; but I mean to put it straight.

STUDDENHAM. I'm a little deaf. Did you say—my daughter?

SIR WILLIAM. There's no use mincing matters, Studdenham. It's a thunderbolt—young Dunning's case over again.

STUDDENHAM. I don't rightly follow. She's— You've—! I must see my daughter. Have the goodness to send for her, m'lady.

    [LADY CHESHIRE *goes to the billiard-room, and calls:* "Freda, come here, please."

STUDDENHAM. [*To* SIR WILLIAM] You tell me that my daughter's in the position of that girl owing to your son? Men ha' been shot for less.

BILL. If you like to have a pot at me, Studenham—you're welcome.

STUDDENHAM. [*Averting his eyes from* BILL *at the sheer idiocy of this sequel to his words*] I've been in your service five and twenty years, Sir William; but this is man to man—this is !

SIR WILLIAM. I don't deny that, Studenham.

STUDDENHAM. [*With eyes shifting in sheer anger*] No—'twouldn't be very easy. Did I understand him to say that he offers her marriage?

SIR WILLIAM. You did.

STUDDENHAM. [*Into his beard*] Well—that's something ! [*Moving his hands as if wringing the neck of a bird.*] I'm trying to see the rights o' this.

SIR WILLIAM. [*Bitterly*] You've all your work cut out for you, Studenham.

    [*Again* STUDDENHAM *makes the unconscious wringing movement with his hands.*

LADY CHESHIRE. [*Turning from it with a sort of horror*] Don't, Studenham. Please !

STUDDENHAM. What's that, m'lady?

LADY CHESHIRE. [*Under her breath*] Your—your—hands.

    [*While* STUDDENHAM *is still staring at her,* FREDA *is seen standing in the doorway, like a black ghost.*

STUDDENHAM. Come here! You! [FREDA *moves a few steps towards her father.*] When did you start this?

FREDA. [*Almost inaudibly*] In the summer, father.

LADY CHESHIRE. Don't be harsh to her!

STUDDENHAM. Harsh! [*His eyes again move from side to side as if pain and anger had bewildered them. Then looking sideways at* FREDA, *but in a gentler voice.*] And when did you tell him about—what's come to you?

FREDA. Last night.

STUDDENHAM. Oh! [*With sudden menace.*] You young——! [*He makes a convulsive movement of one hand; then, in the silence, seems to lose grip of his thoughts, and puts his hand up to his head.*] I want to clear me mind a bit—I don't see it plain at all. [*Without looking at* BILL.] 'Tis said there's been an offer of marriage?

BILL. I've made it, I stick to it.

STUDDENHAM. Oh? [*With slow, puzzled anger.*] I want time to get the pith o' this. You don't say anything, Sir William?

SIR WILLIAM. The facts are all before you.

STUDDENHAM. [*Scarcely moving his lips*] M'lady?

                      [LADY CHESHIRE *is silent.*

STUDDENHAM. [*Stammering*] My girl was—was good enough for any man. It's not for him that's—that's—to look down on her. [*To* FREDA.] You hear the handsome offer that's been made you? Well? [FREDA *moistens her lips and tries to speak, but cannot.*] If nobody's to speak a word, we won't get much forrarder. I'd like for you to say what's in your mind, Sir William.

SIR WILLIAM. I—If my son marries her he'll have to make his own way.

STUDDENHAM. [*Savagely*] I'm not puttin' thought to that.

E

SIR WILLIAM. I didn't suppose you were, Studdenham. It appears to rest with your daughter. [*He suddenly takes out his handkerchief, and puts it to his forehead.*] Infernal fires they make up here!

[LADY CHESHIRE, *who is again shivering desperately, as if with intense cold, makes a violent attempt to control her shuddering.*

STUDDENHAM. [*Suddenly*] There's luxuries that's got to be paid for. [*To* FREDA.] Speak up, now.

[FREDA *turns slowly and looks up at* SIR WILLIAM; *he involuntarily raises his hand to his mouth. Her eyes travel on to* LADY CHESHIRE, *who faces her, but so deadly pale that she looks as if she were going to faint. The girl's gaze passes on to* BILL, *standing rigid, with his jaw set.*

FREDA. I want—[*Then flinging her arm up over her eyes, she turns from him.*] No!

SIR WILLIAM. Ah!

[*At that sound of profound relief,* STUDDENHAM, *whose eyes have been following his daughter's, moves towards* SIR WILLIAM, *all his emotion turned into sheer angry pride.*

STUDDENHAM. Don't be afraid, Sir William! We want none of you! She'll not force herself where she's not welcome. She may ha' slipped her good name, but she'll keep her proper pride. I'll have no *charity marriage* in my family.

SIR WILLIAM. Steady, Studdenham!

STUDDENHAM. If the young gentleman has tired of her in three months, as a blind man can see by the looks of him— she's not for him!

BILL. [*Stepping forward*] I'm ready to make it up to her.

STUDDENHAM. Keep back, there? [*He takes hold of* FREDA, *and looks around him.*] Well! She's not the first this has

happened to since the world began, an' she won't be the last.
Come away, now, come away!

> [*Taking* FREDA *by the shoulders, he guides her towards the
> door.*

SIR WILLIAM. D——n it, Studdenham! Give us credit for
something!

STUDDENHAM. [*Turning—his face and eyes lighted up by a
sort of smiling snarl*] Ah! I do that, Sir William. But there's
things that can't be undone!   [*He follows* FREDA *out.*

> [*As the door closes,* SIR WILLIAM'S *calm gives away. He
> staggers past his wife, and sinks heavily, as though
> exhausted, into a chair by the fire. BILL, following
> FREDA and STUDDENHAM, has stopped at the shut
> door. LADY CHESHIRE moves swiftly close to him.
> The door of the billiard-room is opened, and DOT
> appears. With a glance round, she crosses quickly
> to her mother.*

DOT. [*In a low voice*] Mabel's just going, mother! [*Almost
whispering.*] Where's Freda? Is it—— Has she really had
the pluck?

> [LADY CHESHIRE *bending her head for "Yes," goes out
> into the billiard-room. DOT clasps her hands together
> and standing there in the middle of the room, looks
> from her brother to her father, from her father to her
> brother. A quaint little pitying smile comes on her
> lips. She gives a faint shrug of her shoulders.*

The curtain falls.

THE SKIN GAME

CHARACTERS

HILLCRIST, *a country gentleman*
AMY, *his wife*
JILL, *his daughter*
DAWKER, *his agent*
HORNBLOWER, *a man newly-rich*
CHARLES, *his elder son*
CHLOE, *wife to Charles*
ROLF, *his younger son*
FELLOWS, *Hillcrist's butler*
ANNA, *Chloe's maid*
THE JACKMANS, *man and wife*
  AN AUCTIONEER
  A SOLICITOR
  TWO STRANGERS

ACT I

HILLCRIST'S *study. A pleasant room, with books in calf bindings, and signs that the* HILLCRISTS *have travelled, such as a large photograph of the Taj Mahal, of Table Mountain, and the Pyramids of Egypt. A large bureau [stage Right], devoted to the business of a country estate. Two foxes' masks. Flowers in bowls. Deep armchairs. A large French window open [at Back], with a lovely view of a slight rise of fields and trees in August sunlight. A fine stone fireplace [stage Left]. A door [Left]. A door opposite [Right]. General colour effect—stone, and cigar-leaf brown, with spots of bright colour.*

HILLCRIST *sits in a swivel chair at the bureau, busy with papers. He has gout, and his left foot is encased accordingly. He is a thin, dried-up man of about fifty-five, with a rather refined, rather kindly, and rather cranky countenance. Close to him stands his very upstanding nineteen-year-old daughter* JILL, *with clubbed hair round a pretty, manly face.*

JILL. You know, Dodo, it's all pretty good rot in these days.

HILLCRIST. Cads are cads, Jill, even in these days.

JILL. What is a cad?

HILLCRIST. A self-assertive fellow, without a sense of other people.

JILL. Well, Old Hornblower I'll give you.

HILLCRIST. I wouldn't take him.

JILL. Well, you've got him. Now, Charlie—Chearlie—I say—the importance of not being Charlie——

HILLCRIST. Good heavens! do you know their Christian names?

135

JILL. My dear father, they've been here seven years.

HILLCRIST. In old days we only knew their Christian names from their tombstones.

JILL. Charlie Hornblower isn't really half a bad sport.

HILLCRIST. About a quarter of a bad sport—I've always thought out hunting.

JILL. [*Pulling his hair*] Now, his wife—Chloe——

HILLCRIST. [*Whimsical*] Gad! your mother'd have a fit if she knew you called her Chloe.

JILL. It's a ripping name.

HILLCRIST. Chloe! H'm! I had a spaniel once——

JILL. Dodo, you're narrow. Buck up, old darling, it won't do. Chloe has seen life, I'm pretty sure; *that's* attractive, anyway. No, mother's not in the room; don't turn your uneasy eyes.

HILLCRIST. Really, my dear, you are getting——

JILL. The limit. Now, Rolf——

HILLCRIST. What's Rolf? Another dog?

JILL. Rolf Hornblower's a topper; he really is a nice boy.

HILLCRIST. [*With a sharp look*] Oh! He's a nice boy?

JILL. Yes, darling. You know what a nice boy is, don't you?

HILLCRIST. Not in these days.

JILL. Well, I'll tell you. In the first place, he's not amorous——

HILLCRIST. What! Well, that's some comfort.

JILL. Just a jolly good companion.

HILLCRIST. To whom?

JILL. Well, to anyone—me.

HILLCRIST. Where?

JILL. Anywhere. You don't suppose I confine myself to the home paddocks, do you? I'm naturally rangey, Father.

HILLCRIST. [*Ironically*] You don't say so!

JILL. In the second place, he doesn't like discipline.

HILLCRIST. Jupiter! He does seem attractive.

JILL. In the third place, he bars his father.

HILLCRIST. Is that essential to nice *girls* too?

JILL. [*With a twirl of his hair*] Fish not! Fourthly, he's got ideas.

HILLCRIST. I knew it!

JILL. For instance, he thinks—as I do——

HILLCRIST. Ah! *Good* ideas.

JILL. [*Pulling gently*] Careful! He thinks old people run the show too much. He says they oughtn't to, because they're so damtouchy. Are you damtouchy, darling?

HILLCRIST. Well, I'm——! I don't know about touchy.

JILL. He says there'll be no world fit to live in till we get rid of the old. We must make them climb a tall tree, and shake them off it.

HILLCRIST. [*Dryly*] Oh! he says that!

JILL. Otherwise, with the way they stand on each other's rights, they'll spoil the garden for the young.

HILLCRIST. Does his father agree?

JILL. Oh! Rolf doesn't talk to *him*, his mouth's too large. Have you ever seen it, Dodo?

HILLCRIST. Of course.

JILL. It's considerable, isn't it? Now yours is—reticent, darling. [*Rumpling his hair.*

HILLCRIST. It won't be in a minute. Do you realize that I've got gout?

JILL. Poor ducky! How long have we been here, Dodo?

HILLCRIST. Since Elizabeth, anyway.

JILL. [*Looking at his foot*] It has its drawbacks. D'you think Hornblower had a father? I believe he was spontaneous. But, Dodo, why all this—this *attitude* to the Hornblowers?

[*She purses her lips and makes a gesture as of pushing persons away.*]

HILLCRIST. Because they're pushing.

JILL. That's only because we *are*, as mother would say, and they're *not*—yet. But why not let them be?

HILLCREST. You can't.

JILL. *Why?*

HILLCREST. It takes generations to learn to live and let live, Jill. People like that take an ell when you give them an inch.

JILL. But if you gave them the ell, they wouldn't want the inch. Why should it all be such a skin game?

HILLCREST. Skin game? Where *do* you get your lingo?

JILL. Keep to the point, Dodo.

HILLCREST. Well, Jill, all life's a struggle between people at different stages of development, in different positions, with different amounts of social influence and property. And the only thing is to have rules of the game and keep them. New people like the Hornblowers haven't learnt those rules; *their* only rule is to get all they can.

JILL. Darling, don't prose. They're not half as bad as you think.

HILLCREST. Well, when I sold Hornblower Longmeadow and the cottages, I certainly found him all right. All the same, he's got the cloven hoof. [*Warming up.*] His influence in Deepwater is thoroughly bad; those potteries of his are demoralizing—the whole atmosphere of the place is changing. It was a thousand pities he ever came here and discovered that clay. He's brought in the modern cut-throat spirit.

JILL. Cut *our* throat spirit, you mean. What's your definition of a gentleman, Dodo?

HILLCREST. [*Uneasily*] Can't describe—only feel it.

JILL. Oh! Try!

HILLCREST. Well—er—I suppose you might say—a man who keeps his form and doesn't let life scupper him out of his standards.

JILL. But suppose his standards are low?

HILLCREST. [*With some earnestness*] I assume, of course, that he's honest and tolerant, gentle to the weak, and not self-seeking.

JILL. Ah! self-seeking? But aren't we all, Dodo? *I* am.

HILLCRIST. [*With a smile*] You!

JILL. [*Scornfully*] Oh! yes—too young to know.

HILLCRIST. Nobody knows till they're under pretty heavy fire, Jill.

JILL. Except, of course, mother.

HILLCRIST. How do you mean—mother?

JILL. Mother reminds me of England according to herself—always right whatever she does.

HILLCRIST. Ye-es. Your mother *is* perhaps—the perfect woman——

JILL. That's what I was saying. Now, no one could call *you* perfect, Dodo. Besides, you've got gout.

HILLCRIST. Yes; and I want Fellows. Ring that bell.

JILL. [*Crossing to the bell*] Shall I tell you *my* definition of a gentleman? A man who gives the Hornblower his due. [*She rings the bell.*] And I think mother ought to call on them. Rolf says old Hornblower resents it fearfully that she's never made a sign to Chloe the three years she's been here.

HILLCRIST. I don't interfere with your mother in such matters. She may go and call on the devil himself if she likes.

JILL. I know you're ever so much better than she is.

HILLCRIST. That's respectful.

JILL. You do keep your prejudices out of your phiz. But mother literally looks down her nose. And she never forgives an " h." They'd get the " hell " from her if they took the " hinch."

HILLCRIST. Jill—your language!

JILL. Don't slime out of it, Dodo. I say, mother ought to call on the Hornblowers.   [*No answer.*]
Well?

HILLCRIST. My dear, I always let people have the last word. It makes them—feel funny. Ugh! My foot!

[*Enter* FELLOWS, *Left.*]

Fellows, send into the village and get another bottle of this stuff.

JILL. I'll go, darling.

[*She blows him a kiss, and goes out at the window.*

HILLCRIST. And tell cook I've got to go on slops. This foot's worse.

FELLOWS. [*Sympathetic*] Indeed, sir.

HILLCRIST. My third go this year, Fellows.

FELLOWS. Very annoying, sir.

HILLCRIST. Ye—es. Ever had it?

FELLOWS. I fancy I have had a twinge, sir.

HILLCRIST. [*Brightening*] Have you? Where?

FELLOWS. In my cork wrist, sir.

HILLCRIST. Your what?

FELLOWS. The wrist I draw corks with.

HILLCRIST. [*With a cackle*] You'd have had more than a twinge if you'd lived with my father. H'm!

FELLOWS. Excuse me, sir—Vichy water corks, in my experience, are worse than any wine.

HILLCRIST. [*Ironically*] Ah! The country's not what it was, is it, Fellows?

FELLOWS. Getting very new, sir.

HILLCRIST. [*Feelingly*] You're right. Has Dawker come?

FELLOWS. Not yet, sir. The Jackmans would like to see you, sir.

HILLCRIST. What about?

FELLOWS. I don't know, sir.

HILLCRIST. Well, show them in.

FELLOWS. [*Going*] Yes, sir.

[HILLCRIST *turns his swivel chair round. The* JACKMANS *come in. He, a big fellow about fifty, in a labourer's dress, with eyes which have more in them than his tongue can express; she, a little woman with a worn face, a bright, quick glance, and a tongue to match.*

HILLCRIST. Good morning, Mrs. Jackman! Morning,

Jackman! Haven't seen you for a long time. What can I do? [*He draws in foot, and breath, with a sharp hiss.*

JACKMAN. [*In a down-hearted voice*] We've had notice to quit, sir.

HILLCRIST. [*With emphasis*] What!

JACKMAN. Got to be out this week.

MRS. J. Yes, sir, indeed.

HILLCRIST. Well, but when I sold Longmeadow and the cottages, it was on the express understanding that there was to be no disturbance of tenancies.

MRS. J. Yes, sir; but we've all go to go. Mrs. 'Arvey, and the Drews, an' us, and there isn't another cottage to be had anywhere in Deepwater.

HILLCRIST. I know; I want one for my cowman. This won't do at all. Where do you get it from?

JACKMAN. Mr. 'Ornblower 'imself, sir. Just an hour ago. He come round and said: "I'm sorry; I want the cottages, and you've got to clear."

MRS. J. [*Bitterly*] He's no gentleman, sir; he put it so brisk. We been there thirty years, and now we don't know what to do. So I hope you'll excuse us coming round, sir.

HILLCRIST. I should think so, indeed! H'm! [*He rises and limps across to the fireplace on his stick. To himself.*] The cloven hoof. By George! this is a breach of faith. I'll write to him, Jackman. Confound it! I'd certainly never have sold if I'd known he was going to do this.

MRS. J. No, sir, I'm sure, sir. They do say it's to do with the potteries. He wants the cottages for his workmen.

HILLCRIST. [*Sharply*] That's all very well, but he shouldn't have led me to suppose that he would make no change.

JACKMAN. [*Heavily*] They talk about his havin' bought the Centry to put up more chimneys there, and that's why he wants the cottages.

HILLCRIST. The Centry! Impossible!

MRS. J. Yes, sir; it's such a pretty spot—looks beautiful

from here. [*She looks out through the window.*] Loveliest spot in all Deepwater, I always say. And your father owned it, and his father before 'im. It's a pity they ever sold it, sir, beggin' your pardon.

HILLCRIST. The Centry!   [*He rings the bell.*

MRS. J. [*Who has brightened up*] I'm glad you're goin' to stop it, sir. It does put us about. We don't know where to go. I said to Mr. Hornblower, I said, "I'm sure Mr. Hillcrist would never 'ave turned us out." An' 'e said: "Mr. Hillcrist be —— " beggin' your pardon, sir. "Make no mistake," 'e said, "you must go, missis." He don't even know our name; an' to come it like this over us! He's a dreadful new man, I think, with his overridin' notions. And sich a heavy-footed man, to look at. [*With a sort of indulgent contempt.*] But he's from the North, they say.

[FELLOWS *has entered,* Left.

HILLCRIST. Ask Mrs. Hillcrist if she'll come.

FELLOWS. Very good, sir.

HILLCRIST. Is Dawker here?

FELLOWS. Not yet, sir.

HILLCRIST. I want to see him at once.   [FELLOWS *retires.*

JACKMAN. Mr. Hornblower said he was comin' on to see you, sir. So we thought we'd step along first.

HILLCRIST. Quite right, Jackman.

MRS. J. I said to Jackman: "Mr. Hillcrist'll stand up for us, I know. He's a gentleman," I said. "This man," I said, "don't care for the neighbourhood, or the people; he don't care for anything so long as he makes his money, and has his importance. You can't expect it, I suppose," I said; [*Bitterly*] "havin' got rich so sudden." The gentry don't do things like that.

HILLCRIST. [*Abstracted*] Quite, Mrs. Jackman, quite! [*To himself.*] The Centry! No!

[MRS. HILLCRIST *enters. A well-dressed woman, with a firm, clear-cut face.*]

Oh! Amy! Mr. and Mrs. Jackman turned out of their cottage, and Mrs. Harvey, and the Drews. When I sold to Hornblower, I stipulated that they shouldn't be.

MRS. J. Our week's up on Saturday, ma'am, and I'm sure I don't know where we shall turn, because of course Jackman must be near his work, and I shall lose me washin' if we have to go far.

HILLCRIST. [*With decision*] You leave it to me, Mrs. Jackman. Good morning! Morning, Jackman! Sorry I can't move with this gout.

MRS. J. [*For them both*] I'm sure we're very sorry, sir. Good morning, sir. Good morning, ma'am; and thank you kindly. [*They go out.*

HILLCRIST. Turning people out that have been there thirty years. I won't have it. It's a breach of faith.

MRS. H. Do you suppose this Hornblower will care two straws about that, Jack?

HILLCRIST. He must, when it's put to him, if he's got any decent feeling.

MRS. H. He hasn't.

HILLCRIST. [*Suddenly*] The Jackmans talk of his having bought the Centry to put up more chimneys.

MRS. H. Never! [*At the window, looking out.*] Impossible! It would ruin the place utterly, besides cutting us off from the Duke's. Oh, no! Miss Mullins would never sell behind our backs.

HILLCRIST. Anyway I must stop his turning these people out.

MRS. H. [*With a little smile, almost contemptuous*] You might have known he'd do something of the sort. You will imagine people are like yourself, Jack. You always ought to make Dawker have things in black and white.

HILLCRIST. I said quite distinctly: "Of course you won't want to disturb the tenancies; there's a great shortage of cottages." Hornblower told me as distinctly that he wouldn't. What more do you want?

MRS. H. A man like that thinks of nothing but the short cut to his own way. [*Looking out of the window towards the rise.*] If he buys the Centry and puts up chimneys, we simply couldn't stop here.

HILLCRIST. My father would turn in his grave.

MRS. H. It would have been more useful if he'd not dipped the estate, and sold the Centry. This Hornblower hates us; he thinks we turn up our noses at him.

HILLCRIST. As we do, Amy.

MRS. H. Who wouldn't? A man without traditions, who believes in nothing but money and push.

HILLCRIST. Suppose he won't budge, can we do anything for the Jackmans?

MRS. H. There are the two rooms Beaver used to have, over the stables.   [FELLOWS *enters.*

FELLOWS. Mr. Dawker, sir.

[DAWKER *is a short, square, rather red-faced terrier of a man, in riding clothes and gaiters.*

HILLCRIST. Ah! Dawker, I've got gout again.

DAWKER. Very sorry, sir. How de do, ma'am?

HILLCRIST. Did you meet the Jackmans?

DAWKER. Yeh.

[*He hardly ever quite finishes a word, seeming to snap off their tails.*

HILLCRIST. Then you heard?

DAWKER. [*Nodding*] Smart man, Hornblower; never lets grass grow.

HILLCRIST. Smart?

DAWKER. [*Grinning*] Don't do to underrate your neighbours.

MRS. H. A cad—I call him.

DAWKER. That's it, ma'am—got all the advantage.

HILLCRIST. Heard anything about the Centry, Dawker?

DAWKER. Hornblower wants to buy.

HILLCRIST. Miss Mullins would never sell, would she?

DAWKER. She wants to.

HILLCRIST. The deuce she does!

DAWKER. He won't stick at the price either.

MRS. H. What's it worth, Dawker?

DAWKER. Depends on what you want it for.

MRS. H. He wants it for spite; we want it for sentiment.

DAWKER. [*Grinning*] Worth what you like to give, then; but he's a rich man.

MRS. H. Intolerable!

DAWKER. [*To* HILLCRIST] Give me your figure, sir. I'll try the old lady before he gets at her.

HILLCRIST. [*Pondering*] I don't want to buy, unless there's nothing else for it. I should have to raise the money on the estate; it won't stand much more. I can't believe the fellow would be such a barbarian. Chimneys within three hundred yards, right in front of this house! It's a nightmare.

MRS. H. You'd much better let Dawker make sure, Jack.

HILLCRIST. [*Uncomfortable*] Jackman says Hornblower's coming round to see me. I shall put it to him.

DAWKER. Make him keener than ever. Better get in first.

HILLCRIST. Ape his methods!—Ugh! Confound this gout! [*He gets back to his chair with difficulty.*] Look here, Dawker, I wanted to see you about gates——

FELLOWS. [*Entering*] Mr. Hornblower.

> [HORNBLOWER *enters—a man of medium height, thoroughly broadened, blown out, as it were, by success. He has thick, coarse dark hair, just grizzled, very bushy eyebrows, a wide mouth. He wears quite ordinary clothes, as if that department were in charge of someone who knew about such things. He has a small rose in his buttonhole, and carries a Homburg hat, which one suspects will look too small on his head.*

HORNBLOWER. Good morning! good morning! How are ye, Dawker? Fine morning! Lovely weather!

[*His voice has a curious blend in its tone of brass and oil,
        and an accent not quite Scotch nor quite North
        country.*]

Haven't seen ye for a long time, Hillcrist.

HILLCRIST. [*Who has risen*] Not since I sold you Long-meadow and those cottages, I believe.

HORNBLOWER. Dear me, now! that's what I came about.

HILLCRIST. [*Subsiding again into his chair*] Forgive me! Won't you sit down?

HORNBLOWER. [*Not sitting*] Have ye got gout? That's unfortunate.' I never get it. I've no disposition that way. Had no ancestors, you see. Just me own drinkin' to answer for.

HILLCRIST. You're lucky.

HORNBLOWER. I wonder if Mrs. Hillcrist thinks that! Am I lucky to have no past, ma'am? Just the future?

MRS. H. You're sure you have the future, Mr. Horn-blower?

HORNBLOWER. [*With a laugh*] That's your aristocratic rapier-thrust. You aristocrats are very hard people underneath your manners. Ye love to lay a body out. But I've got the future all right.

HILLCRIST. [*Meaningly*] I've had the Jackmans here, Mr. Hornblower.

HORNBLOWER. Who are they—man with the little spitfire wife?

HILLCRIST. They're very excellent, good people, and they've been in that cottage quietly thirty years.

HORNBLOWER. [*Throwing out his forefinger—a favourite gesture*] Ah! ye've wanted me to stir ye up a bit. Deep-water needs a bit o' go put into it. There's generally some go where I am. I daresay you wish there'd been no " come."

[*He laughs.*]

MRS. H. We certainly like people to keep their word, Mr. Hornblower.

HILLCRIST. Amy!

HORNBLOWER. Never mind, Hillcrist; takes more than that to upset me.

[MRS. HILLCRIST *exchanges a look with* DAWKER, *who slips out unobserved.*

HILLCRIST. You promised me, you know, not to change the tenancies.

HORNBLOWER. Well, I've come to tell ye that I have. I wasn't expecting to have the need when I bought. Thought the Duke would sell me a bit down there; but devil a bit he will; and now I must have those cottages for my workmen. I've got important works, ye know.

HILLCRIST. [*Getting heated*] The Jackmans have their importance too, sir. Their heart's in that cottage.

HORNBLOWER. Have a sense of proportion, man. My works supply thousands of people, and *my* heart's in *them*. What's more, they make my fortune. I've got ambitions— I'm a serious man. Suppose I were to consider this and that, and every little potty objection—where should I get to?— nowhere!

HILLCRIST. All the same, this sort of thing isn't done, you know.

HORNBLOWER. Not by you because ye've got no need to do it. Here ye are, quite content on what your fathers made for ye. Ye've no ambitions; and ye want other people to have none. How d'ye think your fathers got your land?

HILLCRIST. [*Who has risen*] Not by breaking their word.

HORNBLOWER. [*Throwing out his finger*] Don't ye believe it. They got it by breaking their word and turnin' out Jackmans, if that's their name, all over the place.

MRS. H. That's an insult, Mr. Hornblower.

HORNBLOWER. No; it's a repartee. If ye think so much of these Jackmans, build them a cottage yourselves; ye've got the space.

HILLCRIST. That's beside the point.   You promised me, and I sold on that understanding.

HORNBLOWER. And I bought on the understandin' that I'd get some more land from the Duke.

HILLCRIST. That's nothing to do with me.

HORNBLOWER. Ye'll find it has; because I'm going to have those cottages.

HILLCRIST. Well, I call it simply—[*He checks himself.*]

HORNBLOWER. Look here, Hillcrist, ye've not had occasion to understand men like me.   I've got the guts, and I've got the money, and I don't sit still on it.   I'm going ahead because I believe in meself.   I've no use for sentiment and that sort of thing.   Forty of your Jackmans aren't worth me little finger.

HILLCRIST. [*Angry*] Of all the blatant things I ever heard said!——

HORNBLOWER. Well, as we're speaking plainly, I've been thinkin'.   Ye want the village run your old-fashioned way, and I want it run mine.   I fancy there's not room for the two of us here.

MRS. H. When are you going?

HORNBLOWER. Never fear, *I'm* not going.

HILLCRIST. Look here, Mr. Hornblower—this infernal gout makes me irritable—puts me at a disadvantage.   But I should be glad if you'd kindly explain yourself.

HORNBLOWER. [*With a great smile*] Ca' canny; I'm fra' the North.

HILLCRIST. I'm told you wish to buy the Centry and put more of your chimneys up there, regardless of the fact [*He points through the window*] that it would utterly ruin the house we've had for generations, and all our pleasure here.

HORNBLOWER. How the man talks! Why! Ye'd think he owned the sky, because his fathers built him a house with a pretty view, where he's nothing to do but live.   It's sheer want of something to do that gives ye your fine sentiments, Hillcrist.

HILLCRIST. Have the goodness not to charge me with idleness. Dawker—where is he?—[*He shows the bureau.*] When you do the drudgery of your works as thoroughly as I do that of my estate—— Is it true about the Centry?

HORNBLOWER. Gospel true. If ye want to know, my son Chearlie is buyin' it this very minute.

MRS. H. [*Turning with a start*] What do you say?

HORNBLOWER. Ay, he's with the old lady; she wants to sell, an' she'll get her price, whatever it is.

HILLCRIST. [*With deep anger*] If that isn't a skin game, Mr. Hornblower, I don't know what is.

HORNBLOWER. Ah! Ye've got a very nice expression there. "Skin game!" Well, bad words break no bones, an' they're wonderful for hardenin' the heart. If it wasn't for a lady's presence, I could give ye a specimen or two.

MRS. H. Oh! Mr. Hornblower, that need not stop you, I'm sure.

HORNBLOWER. Well, and I don't know that it need. Ye're an obstruction—the like of you—ye're in my path. And anyone in my path doesn't stay there long; or, if he does, he stays there on my terms. And my terms are chimneys in the Centry where I need 'em. It'll do ye a power of good, too, to know that ye're not almighty.

HILLCRIST. And that's being neighbourly!

HORNBLOWER. And how have ye tried bein' neighbourly to me? If I haven't a wife, I've got a daughter-in-law. Have ye called on her, ma'am? I'm new, and ye're an old family. Ye don't like me, ye think I'm a pushin' man. I go to chapel, an' ye don't like that. I make things and I sell them, and ye don't like that. I buy land, and ye don't like that. It threatens the view from your windies. Well, I don't like you, and I'm not goin' to put up with your attitude. Ye've had things your own way too long, and now ye're not going to have them any longer.

HILLCRIST. Will you hold to your word over those cottages?

HORNBLOWER. I'm goin' to have the cottages. I need them, and more besides, now I'm to put up me new works.

HILLCRIST. That's a declaration of war.

HORNBLOWER. Ye never said a truer word. It's one or the other of us, and I rather think it's goin' to be me. I'm the risin' and you're the settin' sun, as the poet says.

HILLCRIST. [*Touching the bell*] We shall see if you can ride rough-shod like this. We used to have decent ways of going about things here. You want to change all that. Well, we shall do our damnedest to stop you. [*To* FELLOWS *at the door.*] Are the Jackmans still in the house? Ask them to be good enough to come in.

HORNBLOWER. [*With the first sign of uneasiness*] I've seen these people. I've nothing more to say to them. I told 'em I'd give 'em five pounds to cover their moving.

HILLCRIST. It doesn't occur to you that people, however humble, like to have some say in their own fate?

HORNBLOWER. I never had any say in mine till I had the brass, and nobody ever will. It's all hypocrisy. You country folk are fair awful hypocrites. Ye talk about good form and all that sort o' thing. It's just the comfortable doctrine of the man in the saddle; sentimental varnish. Ye're every bit as hard as I am, underneath.

MRS. H. [*Who has been standing very still all this time*] You flatter us.

HORNBLOWER. Not at all. God helps those who 'elp themselves—that's at the bottom of all religion. I'm goin' to help meself, and God's going to help me.

MRS. H. I admire your knowledge.

HILLCRIST. We are in the right, and God helps——

HORNBLOWER. Don't ye believe it; ye 'aven't got the energy.

MRS. H. Nor perhaps the conceit.

HORNBLOWER. [*Throwing out his forefinger*] No, no; 'tisn't conceit to believe in yourself when ye've got reason to.

[*The* JACKMANS *have entered.*

HILLCRIST. I'm very sorry, Mrs. Jackman, but I just wanted you to realize that I've done my best with this gentleman.

MRS. J. [*Doubtfully*] Yes, sir. I thought if you spoke for us, he'd feel different-like.

HORNBLOWER. One cottage is the same as another, missis. I made ye a fair offer of five pounds for the moving.

JACKMAN. [*Slowly*] We wouldn't take fifty to go out of that 'ouse. We brought up three children there, an' buried two from it.

MRS. J. [*To* MRS. HILLCRIST] We're attached to it like, ma'am.

HILLCRIST. [*To* HORNBLOWER] How would you like being turned out of a place you were fond of?

HORNBLOWER. Not a bit. But little considerations have to give way to big ones. Now, missis, I'll make it ten pounds, and I'll send a wagon to shift your things. If that isn't fair——! Ye'd better accept, I shan't keep it open.

[*The* JACKMANS *look at each other; their faces show deep anger—and the question they ask each other is which will speak.*

MRS. J. We won't take it; eh, George?

JACKMAN. Not a farden. We come there when we was married.

HORNBLOWER. [*Throwing out his finger*] Ye're very improvident folk.

HILLCRIST. Don't lecture them, Mr. Hornblower; they come out of this miles above you.

HORNBLOWER. [*Angry*] Well, I *was* going to give ye another week, but ye'll go out next Saturday; and take care ye're not late, or your things'll be put out—in the rain.

MRS. H. [*To* MRS. JACKMAN] We'll send down for your things, and you can come to us for the time being.

[MRS. JACKMAN *drops a curtsey; her eyes stab* HORN-
BLOWER.

JACKMAN. [*Heavily, clenching his fists*] You're no gentleman! Don't put temptation in my way, that's all.

HILLCRIST. [*In a low voice*] Jackman!

HORNBLOWER. [*Triumphantly*] Ye hear that? That's your
protégé! Keep out o' *my* way, me man, or I'll put the police
on to ye for utterin' threats.

HILLCRIST. You'd better go now, Jackman.

[*The* JACKMANS *move to the door.*

MRS. J. [*Turning*] Maybe you'll repent it some day, sir.

[*They go out,* MRS. HILLCRIST *following.*

HORNBLOWER. We—ell, I'm sorry they're such unreason-
able folk. I never met people with less notion of which side
their bread was buttered.

HILLCRIST. And I never met anyone so pachydermatous.

HORNBLOWER. What's that, in Heaven's name? Ye
needn't wrap it up in long words now your good lady's
gone.

HILLCRIST. [*With dignity*] I'm not going in for a slanging
match. I resent your conduct much too deeply.

HORNBLOWER. Look here, Hillcrist, I don't object to you
personally; ye seem to me a poor creature that's bound to
get left with your gout and your dignity; but of course ye
can make yourself very disagreeable before ye're done. Now
I want to be the movin' spirit here. I'm full of plans. I'm
goin' to stand for Parliament; I'm goin' to make this a
prosperous place. I'm a good-natured man if you'll treat
me as such. Now, you take me on as a neighbour and all
that, and I'll manage without chimneys on the Centry. Is it
a bargain? [*He holds out his hand.*

HILLCRIST. [*Ignoring it*] I thought you said you didn't keep
your word when it suited you to break it?

HORNBLOWER. Now, don't get on the high horse. You
and me could be very good friends; but I can be a very nasty

enemy. The chimneys will not look nice from that windie, ye know.

HILLCRIST. [*Deeply angry*] Mr. Hornblower, if you think I'll take your hand after this Jackman business, you're greatly mistaken. You are proposing that I shall stand in with you while you tyrannize over the neighbourhood. Please realize that unless you leave those tenancies undisturbed as you said you would, we don't know each other.

HORNBLOWER. Well, that won't trouble me much. Now, ye'd better think it over; ye've got gout and that makes ye hasty. I tell ye again : I'm not the man to make an enemy of. Unless ye're friendly, sure as I stand here I'll ruin the look of your place. [*The toot of a car is heard.*] There's my car. I sent Chearlie and his wife in it to buy the Centry. And make no mistake—he's got it in his pocket. It's your last chance, Hillcrist, I'm not averse to you as a man; I think ye're the best of the fossils round here; at least, I think ye can do me the most harm socially. Come now !

[*He holds out his hand again.*

HILLCRIST. Not if you'd bought the Centry ten times over. Your ways are not mine, and I'll have nothing to do with you.

HORNBLOWER. [*Very angry*] Really! Is that so? Very well. Now ye're goin' to learn something, an' it's time ye did. D'ye realize that I'm very nearly round ye? [*He draws a circle clowly in the air.*] I'm at Uphill, the works are here, here's Longmeadow, here's the Centry that I've just bought, there's only the Common left to give ye touch with the world. Now between you and the Common there's the high road. I come out on the high road here to your north, and I shall come out on it there to your west. When I've got me new works up on the Centry, I shall be makin' a trolley track between the works up to the road at both ends, so my goods will be running right round ye. How'll ye like that for a country place?

[*For answer* HILLCRIST, *who is angry beyond the power of
speech, walks, forgetting to use his stick, up to the
French window.   While he stands there, with his
back to* HORNBLOWER, *the door* L. *is flung open,
and* JILL *enters, preceding* CHARLES, *his wife* CHLOE,
and ROLF.   CHARLES *is a goodish-looking, mous-
tached young man of about twenty-eight, with a white
rim to the collar of his waistcoat, and spats.   He has
his hand behind* CHLOE'S *back, as if to prevent her
turning tail.   She is rather a handsome young woman,
with dark eyes, full red lips, and a suspicion of powder,
a little under-dressed for the country.   ROLF, who
brings up the rear, is about twenty, with an open face
and stiffish butter-coloured hair.   JILL runs over to
her father at the window.   She has a bottle.*

JILL. [*Sotto voce*] Look, Dodo, I've brought the lot!   Isn't
it a treat, dear Papa?   And here's the stuff.   Hallo!

*The exclamation is induced by the apprehension that there
has been a row.   HILLCRIST gives a stiff little bow,
remaining where he is in the window.   JILL stays close
to him, staring from one to the other, then blocks
him off and engages him in conversation.   CHARLES
has gone up to his father, who has remained maliciously
still, where he delivered his last speech.   CHLOE and
ROLF stand awkwardly waiting between the fireplace
and the door.*

HORNBLOWER. Well, Chearlie?

CHARLES. Not got it.

HORNBLOWER. *Not* !

CHARLES. I'd practically got her to say she'd sell at three
thousand five hundred, when that fellow Dawker turned up.

HORNBLOWER. That bull-terrier of a chap!   Why, he was
here a while ago.   Oh—ho!   So that's it!

CHARLES. I heard him gallop up.   He came straight for
the old lady, and got her away.   What he said I don't know;

but she came back looking wiser than an owl; said she'd think it over, thought she had other views.

HORNBLOWER. Did ye tell her she might have her price?

CHARLES. Practically I did.

HORNBLOWER. Well?

CHARLES. She thought it would be fairer to put it up to auction. There were other inquiries. Oh! She's a leery old bird—reminds me of one of those pictures of Fate, don't you know.

HORNBLOWER. Auction! Well, if it's not gone we'll get it yet. That damned little Dawker! I've had a row with Hillcrist.

CHARLES. I thought so.

[*They are turning cautiously to look at* HILLCRIST, *when* JILL *steps forward.*

JILL. [*Flushed and determined*] That's not a bit sporting of you, Mr. Hornblower. [*At her words* ROLF *comes forward too.*

HORNBLOWER. Ye should hear both sides before ye say that, missy.

JILL. There isn't another side to turning out the Jackmans after you'd promised.

HORNBLOWER. Oh! dear me, yes. They don't matter a row of gingerbread to the schemes I've got for betterin' this neighbourhood.

JILL. I *had* been standing up for you; now I won't.

HORNBLOWER. Dear, dear! What'll become of me?

JILL. I won't say anything about the other thing because I think it's beneath dignity to notice it. But to turn poor people out of their cottages is a shame.

HORNBLOWER. Hoity me!

ROLF. [*Suddenly*] You haven't been doing that, father?

CHARLES. Shut up, Rolf!

HORNBLOWER. [*Turning on* ROLF] Ha! Here's a league o' youth! My young whipper-snapper, keep your mouth shut and leave it to your elders to know what's right.

[*Under the weight of this rejoinder* ROLF *stands biting his lips. Then he throws his head up.*

ROLF. I hate it!

HORNBLOWER. [*With real venom*] Oh! Ye hate it? Ye can get out of my house, then.

JILL. Free speech, Mr. Hornblower; don't be violent.

HORNBLOWER. Ye're right, young lady. Ye can stay in my house, Rolf, and learn manners. Come, Chearlie!

JILL. [*Quite softly*] Mr. Hornblower!

HILLCRIST. [*From the window*] Jill!

JILL. [*Impatiently*] Well, what's the good of it? Life's too short for rows, and too jolly!

ROLF. Bravo!

HORNBLOWER. [*Who has shown a sign of weakening*] Now, look here! I will not have revolt in my family. Ye'll just have to learn that a man who's worked as I have, who's risen as I have, and who knows the world, is the proper judge of what's right and wrong. I'll answer to God for me actions, and not to you young people.

JILL. Poor God!

HORNBLOWER. [*Genuinely shocked*] Ye blasphemous young thing! [*To* ROLF] And ye're just as bad, ye young free-thinker. I won't have it.

HILLCRIST. [*Who has come down, Right*] Jill, I wish you would kindly not talk.

JILL. I can't help it.

CHARLES. [*Putting his arm through* HORNBLOWER'S] Come along, father! Deeds, not words.

HORNBLOWER. Ay! Deeds!

[MRS. HILLCRIST *and* DAWKER *have entered by the French window.*

MRS. H. Quite right!   [*They all turn and look at her.*

HORNBLOWER. Ah! So ye put your dog on to it. [*He throws out his finger at* DAWKER.] Very smart, that—I give ye credit.

Mrs. H. [*Pointing to* Chloe, *who has stood by herself, forgotten and uncomfortable throughout the scene*] May I ask who this lady is?

> [Chloe *turns round startled, and her vanity bag slips down her dress to the floor.*

Hornblower. No, ma'am, ye may not, for ye know perfectly well.

Jill. I brought her in, mother.

> [*She moves to* Chloe's *side.*

Mrs. H. Will you take her out again, then.

Hillcrist. Amy, have the goodness to remember——

Mrs. H. That this is my house so far as ladies are concerned.

Jill. Mother!

> [*She looks astonished at* Chloe, *who, about to speak, does not, passing her eyes, with a queer, half-scared expression, from* Mrs. Hillcrist *to* Dawker.]

[*To* Chloe.] I'm awfully sorry. Come on!

> [*They go out, Left.* Rolf *hurries after them.*

Charles. You've insulted my wife. Why? What do you mean by it?   [Mrs. Hillcrist *simply smiles.*

Hillcrist. I apologize. I regret extremely. There is no reason why the ladies of your family or of mine should be involved in our quarrel. For Heaven's sake, let's fight like gentlemen.

Hornblower. Catchwords—sneers! No; we'll play what ye call a skin game, Hillcrist, without gloves on; we won't spare each other. Ye look out for yourselves, for, begod, after this morning I mean business. And as for you, Dawker, ye sly dog, ye think yourself very clever; but I'll have the Centry yet. Come, Chearlie.

> [*They go out, passing* Jill, *who is coming in again, in the doorway.*

Hillcrist. Well, Dawker?

Dawker. [*Grinning*] Safe for the moment. The old lady'll

put it up to auction.   Couldn't get her to budge from that.
Says she don't want to be unneighbourly to either.   But, if
you ask me, it's money she smells!

JILL [*Advancing*] Now, mother!

MRS. H. Well?

JILL. Why did you insult her?

MRS. H. I think I only asked you to take her out.

JILL. Why? Even if she is Old Combustion's daughter-
in-law?

MRS. H. My dear Jill, allow me to judge the sort of
acquaintances I wish to make.   [*She looks at* DAWKER.

JILL. She's all right.   Lots of women powder and touch
up their lips nowadays.   I think she's rather a good sort; she
was awfully upset.

MRS. H. Too upset.

JILL. Oh! don't be so mysterious, mother.   If you know
something, do spit it out!

MRS. H. Do you wish me to—er—"spit it out," Jack?

HILLCRIST. Dawker, if you don't mind——

[DAWKER, *with a nod, passes away out of the French
window.*]

Jill, be respectful, and don't talk like a bargee.

JILL. It's no good, Dodo. It made me ashamed. Its
just as—as caddish to insult people who haven't said a word,
in your own house, as it is to be—old Hornblower.

MRS. H. You don't know what you're talking about.

HILLCRIST. What's the matter with young Mrs. Hornblower?

MRS. H. Excuse me, I shall keep my thoughts to myself at
present.

[*She looks coldly at* JILL, *and goes out through the French
window.*

HILLCRIST. You've thoroughly upset your mother, Jill.

JILL. It's something Dawker's told her; I saw them. I
don't like Dawker, father, he's so common.

HILLCRIST. My dear, we can't all be uncommon. He's got lots of go. You must apologize to your mother.

JILL. [*Shaking her clubbed hair*] They'll make you do things you don't approve of, Dodo, if you don't look out. Mother's fearfully bitter when she gets her knife in. If old Hornblower's disgusting, it's no reason we should be.

HILLCRIST. So you think I'm capable—that's nice, Jill!

JILL. No, no, darling! I only want to warn you solemnly that mother'll tell you you're fighting fair, no matter what she and Dawker do.

HILLCRIST. [*Smiling*] Jill, I don't think I ever saw you so serious.

JILL. No. Because—[*She swallows a lump in her throat.*] Well—I was just beginning to enjoy myself; and now—everything's going to be bitter and beastly, with mother in that mood. That horrible old man! Oh, Dodo! Don't let them make *you* horrid! You're such a darling. How's your gout, ducky?

HILLCRIST. Better; lot better.

JILL. There, you see! That shows! It's going to be half interesting for you, but not for—us.

HILLCRIST. Look here, Jill—is there anything between you and young what's-his-name—Rolf?

JILL. [*Biting her lip*] No. But—now it's *all* spoiled

HILLCRIST. You can't expect me to regret that.

JILL. I don't mean any tosh about love's young dream; but I do like being friends. I want to *enjoy* things, Dodo, and you can't do that when everybody's on the hate. You're going to wallow in it, and so shall I—oh! I know I shall!—we shall all wallow, and think of nothing but " one for his nob."

HILLCRIST. Aren't you fond of your home?

JILL. Of course. I love it.

HILLCRIST. Well, you won't be able to live in it unless we stop that ruffian. Chimneys and smoke, the trees cut down, piles of pots. Every kind of abomination. There! [*He points.*] Imagine! [*He points through the French window, as if he could see those chimneys rising and marring the beauty of the fields.*] I was born here, and my father, and his, and his, and his. They loved those fields, and those old trees. And this barbarian, with his "improvement" schemes, forsooth! I learned to ride in the Centry meadows—prettiest spring meadows in the world; I've climbed every tree there. Why my father ever sold——! But who could have imagined this? And come at a bad moment, when money's scarce.

JILL. [*Cuddling his arm*] Dodo!

HILLCRIST. Yes. But you don't love the place as I do, Jill. You youngsters don't love anything, I sometimes think.

JILL. I do, Dodo, I do!

HILLCRIST. You've got it all before you. But you may live your life and never find anything so good and so beautiful as this old home. I'm not going to have it spoiled without a fight.

> [*Conscious of having betrayed sentiment, he walks out at the French window, passing away to the Right. JILL, following to the window, looks. Then throwing back her head, she clasps her hands behind it.*

JILL. Oh—oh—oh!

> [*A voice behind her says, "Jill!" She turns and starts back, leaning against the Right lintel of the window. ROLF appears outside the window from Left.*]

Who goes there?

ROLF. [*Buttressed against the Left lintel*] Enemy—after Chloe's bag.

JILL. Pass, enemy! And all's ill!

> [*ROLF passes through the window, and retrieves the vanity bag from the floor where CHLOE dropped it, then again takes his stand against the Left lintel of the French window.*

ROLF. It's not going to make any difference, is it?

JILL. You know it is.

ROLF. Sins of the fathers.

JILL. Unto the third and fourth generation. What sin has *my* father committed?

ROLF. None, in a way; only, I've often told you I don't see why you should treat us as outsiders. We don't like it.

JILL. Well, you shouldn't be, then; I mean, *he* shouldn't be.

ROLF. Father's just as human as your father; he's wrapped up in us, and all his " getting on " is for us. Would you like to be treated as your mother treated Chloe? Your mother's set the stroke for the other big-wigs about here; nobody calls on Chloe. And why not? Why not? I think it's contemptible to bar people just because they're *new*, as you call it, and have to make their position instead of having it left them.

JILL. It's *not* because they're new, it's because—if your father behaved like a gentleman, he'd be treated like one.

ROLF. Would he? I don't believe it. My father's a very able man; he thinks he's entitled to have influence here. Well, everybody tries to keep him down. Oh! yes, they do. That makes him mad and more determined than ever to get his way. You ought to be just, Jill.

JILL. I *am* just.

ROLF. No, you're not. Besides, what's it got to do with Charlie and Chloe? Chloe's particularly harmless. It's pretty sickening for her. Father didn't expect people to call until Charlie married, but since——

JILL. I think it's all very petty.

ROLF. It *is*—a dog-in-the-manger business; I did think *you* were above it.

JILL. How would you like to have your home spoiled?

ROLF. I'm not going to argue. Only things don't stand still. Homes aren't any more proof against change than anything else.

JILL. All right! You come and try and take ours.

F

ROLF. We don't want to take your home.

JILL. Like the Jackmans'?

ROLF. All right.   I see you're hopelessly prejudiced.

[*He turns to go.*

JILL. [*Just as he is vanishing—softly*] Enemy?

ROLF. [*Turning*] Yes, enemy.

JILL. Before the battle—let's shake hands.

[*They move from the lintels and grasp each other's hands in the centre of the French window.*

The curtain falls.

ACT II

SCENE I

A billiard room in a provincial hotel, where things are bought and
sold. The scene is set well forward, and is not very broad;
it represents the auctioneer's end of the room, having, rather
to stage Left, a narrow table with two chairs facing the
audience, where the auctioneer will sit and stand. The table,
which is set forward to the footlights, is littered with green-
covered particulars of sale. The audience are in effect public
and bidders. There is a door on the Left, level with the table.
Along the back wall, behind the table, are two raised benches
with two steps up to them, such as billiard rooms often have,
divided by a door in the middle of a wall, which is panelled in
oak. Late September sunlight is coming from a skylight
(not visible) on to these seats. The stage is empty when the
curtain goes up, but DAWKER *and* MRS. HILLCRIST *are just*
entering through the door at the back.

DAWKER. Be out of their way here, ma'am. See old
Hornblower with Chearlie?

> [*He points down to the audience.*

MRS. H. It begins at three, doesn't it?

DAWKER. They won't be over punctual; there's only the
Centry selling. There's young Mrs. Hornblower with the
other boy—[*Pointing*] over at the entrance. I've got that
chap I told you of down from town.

MRS. H. Ah! make quite sure of her, Dawker. Any
mistake would be fatal.

DAWKER. [*Nodding*] That's right, ma'am. Lot of people—

163

always spare time to watch an auction—ever remark that? The Duke's agent's here; shouldn't be surprised if he chipped in.

MRS. H. Where did you leave my husband?

DAWKER. With Miss Jill, in the courtyard. He's coming to you. In case I miss him, tell him when I reach his limit to blow his nose if he wants me to go on; when he blows it a second time, I'll stop for good. Hope we shan't get to that. Old Hornblower doesn't throw his money away.

MRS. H. What limit did you settle?

DAWKER. Six thousand!

MRS. H. That's a fearful price. Well, good luck to you, Dawker!

DAWKER. Good luck, ma'am. I'll go and see to that little matter of Mrs. Chloe. Never fear, we'll do them in somehow.

[He winks, lays his finger on the side of his nose, and goes out at the door.

[MRS. HILLCRIST mounts the two steps, sits down Right of the door, and puts up a pair of long-handled glasses. Through the door behind her come CHLOE and ROLF. She makes a sign for him to go, and shuts the door.

CHLOE. [At the foot of the steps—in the gangway—in a slightly common accent] Mrs. Hillcrist!

MRS. H. [Not quite starting] I beg your pardon?

CHLOE. [Again] Mrs. Hillcrist——

MRS. H. Well?

CHLOE. I never did you any harm.

MRS. H. Did I ever say you did?

CHLOE. No; but you act as if I had.

MRS. H. I'm not aware that I've acted at all—as yet. You are nothing to me, except as one of your family.

CHLOE. 'Tisn't I that wants to spoil your home.

MRS. H. Stop them, then. I see your husband down there with his father.

CHLOE. I—I have tried.

MRS. H. [*Looking at her*] Oh! I suppose such men don't pay attention to what women ask them.

CHLOE. [*With a flash of spirit*] I'm fond of my husband. I——

MRS. H. [*Looking at her steadily*] I don't quite know why you spoke to me.

CHLOE. [*With a sort of pathetic sullenness*] I only thought perhaps you'd like to treat me as a human being.

MRS. H. Really, if you don't mind, I should like to be left alone just now.

CHLOE. [*Unhappily acquiescent*] Certainly! I'll go to the other end. [*She moves to the Left, mounts the steps and sits down.*

    [ROLF, *looking in through the door, and seeing where she is, joins her.* MRS. HILLCRIST *re-settles herself a little further in on the Right.*

ROLF. [*Bending over to* CHLOE, *after a glance at* MRS. HILLCRIST] Are you all right?

CHLOE. It's awfully hot.

        [*She fans herself with the particulars of sale.*

ROLF. There's Dawker. I hate that chap!

CHLOE. Where?

ROLF. Down there; see?

        [*He points down to stage Right of the room.*

CHLOE. [*Drawing back in her seat with a little gasp*] Oh!

ROLF. [*Not noticing*] Who's that next him, looking up here?

CHLOE. I don't know.

    [*She has raised her auction programme suddenly, and sits fanning herself, carefully screening her face.*

ROLF. [*Looking at her*] Don't you feel well? Shall I get you some water? [*He gets up at her nod.*

    [*As he reaches the door,* HILLCRIST *and* JILL *come in.* HILLCRIST *passes him abstractedly with a nod, and sits down beside his wife.*

JILL. [*To* ROLF] Come to see us turned out?

ROLF. [*Emphatically*] No.   I'm looking after Chloe; she's not well.

JILL. [*Glancing at her*] Sorry.   She needn't have come, I suppose?   [ROLF *deigns no answer, and goes out.*

> [JILL *glances at* CHLOE, *then at her parents talking in low voices, and sits down next her father, who makes room for her.*

MRS. H. Can Dawker see you there, Jack? [HILLCRIST *nods.* What's the time?

HILLCRIST. Three minutes to three.

JILL. Don't you feel beastly all down the backs of your legs, Dodo?

HILLCRIST. Yes.

JILL. Do you, mother?

MRS. H. No.

JILL. A wagon of old Hornblower's pots passed while we were in the yard.   It's an omen.

MRS. H. Don't be foolish, Jill.

JILL. Look at the old brute!   Dodo, hold my hand.

MRS. H. Make sure you've got a handkerchief, Jack.

HILLCRIST. I can't go beyond the six thousand; I shall have to raise every penny on mortgage as it is.   The estate simply won't stand more, Amy.

> [*He feels in his breast pocket, and pulls up the edge of his handkerchief.*

JILL. Oh!   Look!   There's Miss Mullins, at the back; just come in.   Isn't she a spidery old chip?

MRS. H. Come to gloat.   Really, I think her not accepting your offer is disgusting.   Her impartiality is all humbug.

HILLCRIST. Can't blame her for getting what she can—it's human nature.   Phew!   I used to feel like this before a *vivâ voce*.   Who's that next to Dawker?

JILL. What a fish!

MRS. H. [*To herself*] Ah!   yes.

[*Her eyes slide round at* CHLOE, *sitting motionless and
rather sunk in her seat, slowly fanning herself with the
particulars of the sale.*]

Jack, go and offer her my smelling salts.

HILLCRIST. [*Taking the salts*] Thank God for a human
touch!

MRS. H. [*Taken aback*] Oh! I——

JILL. [*With a quick look at her mother, snatching the salts*] I
will.   [*She goes over to* CHLOE *with the salts.*]
Have a sniff; you look awfully white.

CHLOE. [*Looking up, startled*] Oh! no, thanks. I'm all
right.

JILL. No, do! You must.   [CHLOE *takes them.*

JILL. D'you mind letting me see that a minute?

[*She takes the particulars of the sale and studies it, but
CHLOE has buried the lower part of her face in her hand
and the smelling salts bottle.*]

Beastly hot, isn't it? You'd better keep that.

CHLOE. [*Her dark eyes wandering and uneasy*] Rolf's getting
me some water.

JILL. Why do you stay? You didn't want to come, did
you?   [CHLOE *shakes her head.*]
All right! Here's your water.

[*She hands back the particulars and slides over to her seat,
passing* ROLF *in the gangway, with her chin well up.*

[MRS. HILLCRIST, *who has watched* CHLOE *and* JILL *and*
DAWKER *and his friend, makes an inquiring movement
with her hand, but gets a disappointing answer.*

JILL. What's the time, Dodo?

HILLCRIST. [*Looking at his watch*] Three minutes past.

JILL [*Sighing*] Oh, hell!

HILLCRIST. Jill!

JILL. Sorry, Dodo. I was only thinking. Look! Here
he is! Phew!—isn't he——?

MRS. H. 'Sh!

[*The* AUCTIONEER *comes in Left and goes to the table. He
is a square, short, brown-faced, common-looking man,
with clipped grey hair fitting him like a cap, and a
clipped grey moustache. His lids come down over his
quick eyes, till he can see you very sharply, and you
can hardly see that he can see you. He can break into
a smile at any moment, which has no connection with
him, as it were. By a certain hurt look, however, when
bidding is slow, he discloses that he is not merely an
auctioneer, but has in him elements of the human
being. He can wink with anyone, and is dressed in a
snuff-brown suit, with a perfectly unbuttoned waistcoat, a low, turned-down collar, and small black and
white sailor-knot tie. While he is settling his papers,
the* HILLCRISTS *settle themselves tensely.* CHLOE
*has drunk her water and leaned back again, with the
smelling salts to her nose.* ROLF *leans forward in the
seat beside her, looking sideways at* JILL. *A* SOLICI-
TOR, *with a grey beard, has joined the* AUCTIONEER *at
his table.*

AUCTIONEER. [*Tapping the table*] Sorry to disappoint you,
gentlemen, but I've only one property to offer you to-day,
No. 1, The Centry, Deepwater. The second on the particulars has been withdrawn. The third—that's Bidcot,
desirable freehold mansion and farmlands in the Parish of
Kenway—we shall have to deal with next week. I shall be
happy to sell it you then without reservation. [*He looks again
through the particulars in his hand, giving the audience time to
readjust themselves to his statements.*] Now, gen'lemen, as I
say, I've only the one property to sell. Freehold No. 1—
all that very desirable corn and stock-rearing and parklike
residential land known as the Centry, Deepwater, unique
property—an A 1 chance to an A 1 audience. [*With his
smile.*] Ought to make the price of the three we thought we
had. Now you won't mind listening to the conditions of sale;

Mr. Blinkard'll read 'em, and they won't wirry you, they're very short.

> [*He sits down and gives two little taps on the table.*
> [*The* SOLICITOR *rises and reads the conditions of sale in a voice which no one practically can hear. Just as he begins to read these conditions of sale,* CHARLES HORNBLOWER *enters at back. He stands a moment, glancing round at the* HILLCRISTS *and twirling his moustache, then moves along to his wife and touches her.*

CHARLES. Chloe, aren't you well?

> [*In the start which she gives, her face is fully revealed to the audience.*

CHARLES. Come along, out of the way of these people.

> [*He jerks his head towards the* HILLCRISTS. CHLOE *gives a swift look down to the stage Right of the audience.*

CHLOE. No; I'm all right; it's hotter there.

CHARLES. [*To* ROLF] Well, look after her—I must go back.

> [ROLF *nods.* CHARLES *slides back to the door, with a glance at the* HILLCRISTS, *of whom* MRS. HILLCRIST *has been watching like a lynx. He goes out, just as the* SOLICITOR, *finishing, sits down.*

AUCTIONEER. [*Rising and tapping*] Now, gen'lemen, it's not often a piece of land like this comes into the market. What's that? [*To a friend in front of him.*] No better land in Deepwater—that's right, Mr. Spicer. I know the village well, and a charming place it is; perfect locality, to be sure. Now I don't want to wirry you by singing the praises of this property; there is it—well-watered, nicely timbered—no reservation on the timber, gen'lemen—no tenancy to hold you up; free to do what you like with it to-morrow. You've got a jewel of a site there, too; perfect position for a house. It lies between the Duke's and Squire Hillcrist's—an emerald isle. [*With his smile.*] No allusion to Ireland, gen'lemen— perfect peace in the Centry. Nothing like it in the county— a gen'leman's site, and you don't get that offered you every

day. [*He looks down towards* HORNBLOWER, *stage Left.*]
Carries the mineral rights, and as you know, perhaps, there's
the very valuable Deepwater clay there. What am I to start
it at? Can I say three thousand? Well, anything you like to
give me. I'm not particular. Come now, you've got more
time than me, I expect. Two hundred acres of first-rate
grazin' and cornland, with a site for a residence unequalled
in the county; and all the possibilities? Well, what shall I
say?   [*Bid from* SPICER.]
Two thousand? [*With his smile.*] That won't hurt you, Mr.
Spicer. Why, it's worth that to overlook the Duke. For
two thousand?   [*Bid from* HORNBLOWER, *stage Left.*]
And five. Thank you, sir. Two thousand five hundred
bid.   [*To a friend just below him.*]
Come, Mr. Sandy, don't scratch your head over it.

                          [*Bid from* DAWKER, *stage Right.*]
And five. Three thousand bid for this desirable property.
Why, you'd think it wasn't desirable. Come along, gen'le-
men. A little spirit.   [*A slight pause.*

    JILL. Why can't I *see* the bids, Dodo?
    HILLCRIST. The last was Dawker's.
    AUCTIONEER. For three thousand. [HORNBLOWER.] Three
thousand five hundred? May I say four? [*A bid from the
centre.*] No, I'm not particular; I'll take hundreds. Three
thousand six hundred bid. [HORNBLOWER.] And seven.
Three thousand seven hundred, and——

                    [*He pauses, quartering the audience.*
    JILL. Who was that, Dodo?
    HILLCRIST. Hornblower. It's the Duke in the centre.
    AUCTIONEER. Come, gen'lemen, don't keep me all day.
Four thousand may I say? [DAWKER.] Thank you. We're
beginning. And one? [*A bid from the centre.*] Four thousand
one hundred. [HORNBLOWER.] Four thousand two hundred.
May I have yours, sir? [*To* DAWKER.] And three. Four
thousand three hundred bid. No such site in the county,

gen'lemen. I'm going to sell this land for what it's worth. You can't bid too much for me. [*He smiles.*] [HORNBLOWER.] Four thousand five hundred bid. [*Bid from the centre.*] And six. [DAWKER.] And seven. [HORNBLOWER.] And eight. Nine, may I say? [*But the centre has dried up.*] [DAWKER.] And nine. [HORNBLOWER.] Five thousand. Five thousand bid. That's better; there's some spirit in it. For five thousand. [*He pauses while he speaks to the* SOLICITOR.

HILLCRIST. It's a duel now.

AUCTIONEER. Now, gen'lemen, I'm not going to give this property away. Five thousand bid. [DAWKER.] And one. [HORNBLOWER.] And two. [DAWKER.] And three. Five thousand three hundred bid. And five, did you say, sir? [HORNBLOWER.] Five thousand five hundred bid.

[*He looks at his particulars.*

JILL. [*Rather agonized*] Enemy, Dodo.

AUCTIONEER. This chance may never come again.

> " How you'll regret it
>   If you don't get it,"

as the poet says. May I say five thousand six hundred, sir? [DAWKER.] Five thousand six hundred bid. [HORNBLOWER.] And seven. [DAWKER.] And eight. For five thousand eight hundred pounds. We're gettin' on, but we haven't got the value yet.

[*A slight pause, while he wipes his brow at the success of his own efforts.*

JILL. Us, Dodo?

[HILLCRIST *nods.* JILL *looks over at* ROLF, *whose face is grimly set.* CHLOE *has never moved.* MRS. HILL-CRIST *whispers to her husband.*

AUCTIONEER. Five thousand eight hundred bid. For five thousand eight hundred. Come along, gen'lemen, come along. We're not beaten. Thank you, sir. [HORN-BLOWER.] Five thousand nine hundred. And——? [DAWKER.

Six thousand. Six thousand bid. Six thousand bid. For
six thousand! The Centry—most desirable spot in the
county—going for the low price of six thousand.

HILLCRIST. [*Muttering*] Low! Heavens!

AUCTIONEER. Any advance on six thousand? Come,
gen'lemen, we haven't dried up? A little spirit. Six
thousand? For six thousand? For six thousand pounds?
Very well, I'm selling. For six thousand once—[*He taps.*]
For six thousand twice—[*He taps.*]

JILL. [*Low*] Oh! we've got it!

AUCTIONEER. And one, sir? [HORNBLOWER.] Six thousand
one hundred bid.

> [*The* SOLICITOR *touches his arm and says something, to
> which the* AUCTIONEER *responds with a nod.*

MRS. H. Blow your nose, Jack.

> [HILLCRIST *blows his nose.*

AUCTIONEER. For six thousand one hundred. [DAWKER.]
And two. Thank you. [HORNBLOWER.] And three. For
six thousand three hundred. [DAWKER.] And four. For
six thousand four hundred pounds. This coveted property.
For six thousand four hundred pounds. Why, it's giving it
away, gen'lemen.   [*A pause.*

MRS. H. Giving!

AUCTIONEER. Six thousand four hundred bid.   [HORN-
BLOWER.] And five. [DAWKER.] And six. [HORNBLOWER.]
And seven. [DAWKER.] And eight.

> [*A pause, during which, through the door Left, someone
> beckons to the* SOLICITOR, *who rises and confers.*

HILLCRIST. [*Muttering*] I've done if that doesn't get it.

AUCTIONEER. For six thousand eight hundred. For six
thousand eight hundred—once—[*He taps*] twice—[*He taps.*]
For the last time. This dominating site. [HORNBLOWER.]
And nine. Thank you. For six thousand nine hundred.

> [HILLCRIST *has taken out his handkerchief.*

JILL. Oh! Dodo!

MRS. H. [*Quivering*] Don't give in!

AUCTIONEER. Seven thousand may I say? [DAWKER.] Seven thousand.

MRS. H. [*Whispers*] Keep it down; don't show him.

AUCTIONEER. For seven thousand—going for seven thousand—once—[*Taps*] twice—[*Taps.*] [HORNBLOWER.] And one. Thank you, sir.

> [HILLCRIST *blows his nose.* JILL, *with a choke, leans back in her seat and folds her arms tightly on her chest.* MRS. HILLCRIST *passes her handkerchief over her lips, sitting perfectly still.* HILLCRIST *too is motionless.*
>
> [*The* AUCTIONEER *has paused, and is talking to the* SOLICITOR, *who has returned to his seat.*

MRS. H. Oh! Jack.

JILL. Stick it, Dodo; stick it!

AUCTIONEER. Now, gen'lemen, I have a bid of seven thousand one hundred for the Centry. And I'm instructed to sell if I can't get more. It's a fair price, but not a big price. [*To his friend* MR. SPICER.] A thumpin' price? [*With his smile.*] Well, you're a judge of thumpin', I admit. Now, who'll give me seven thousand two hundred? What, no one? Well, I can't make you, gen'lemen. For seven thousand one hundred. Once—[*Taps.*] Twice—[*Taps.*]

> [JILL *utters a little groan.*

HILLCRIST. [*Suddenly, in a queer voice*] Two.

AUCTIONEER. [*Turning with surprise and looking up to receive* HILLCRIST'S *nod*] Thank you, sir. And two. Seven thousand two hundred. [*He screws himself round so as to command both* HILLCRIST *and* HORNBLOWER.] May I have yours, sir? [HORNBLOWER.] And three. [HILLCRIST.] And four. Seven thousand four hundred. For seven thousand four hundred. [HORNBLOWER.] Five. [HILLCRIST.] Six. For seven thousand six hundred. [*A pause.*] Well, gen'lemen, this is better, but a record property shid fetch a record price. The possibilities are enormous. [HORNBLOWER.] Eight thousand did you say, sir? Eight thousand. Going for eight thousand pounds. [HILLCRIST.] And one. [HORNBLOWER.] And two. [HILLCRIST.] And three. [HORNBLOWER.] And four. [HILLCRIST.] And five. For eight thousand five hundred. A wonderful property for eight thousand five hundred.

[*He wipes his brow.*

JILL. [*Whispering*] Oh, Dodo!

MRS. H. That's enough, Jack, we must stop some time.

AUCTIONEER. For eight thousand five hundred. Once— [*Taps.*] Twice—[*Taps.*] [HORNBLOWER.] Six hundred. [HILLCRIST.] Seven. May I have yours, sir? [HORNBLOWER.] Eight.

HILLCRIST. Nine thousand.

[MRS. HILLCRIST *looks at him, biting her lips, but he is quite absorbed.*

AUCTIONEER. Nine thousand for this astounding property. Why, the Duke would pay that if he realized he'd be overlooked. Now, sir? [*To* HORNBLOWER. *No response.*] Just a little raise on that. [*No response.*] For nine thousand. The Centry, Deepwater, for nine thousand. Once—[*Taps.*] Twice—[*Taps.*]

JILL. [*Under her breath*] Ours!

A VOICE. [*From far back in the centre.*] And five hundred.

AUCTIONEER. [*Surprised and throwing out his arms towards the voice*] And five hundred. For nine thousand five hundred. May I have yours, sir? [*He looks at* HORNBLOWER. *No response.*]   [*The* SOLICITOR *speaks to him.*

MRS. H. [*Whispering*] It must be the Duke again.

HILLCRIST. [*Passing his hand over his brow*] That's stopped him, anyway.

AUCTIONEER. [*Looking at* HILLCRIST] For nine thousand five hundred?   [HILLCRIST *shakes his head.*
Once more. The Centry, Deepwater, for nine thousand five hundred. Once—[*Taps.*] Twice—[*Taps.*] [*He pauses and looks again at* HORNBLOWER *and* HILLCRIST.] For the last time—

at nine thousand five hundred   [*Taps.*] [*With a look towards the bidder.*] Mr. Smalley. Well! [*With great satisfaction.*] That's that! No more to-day, gen'lemen.

> [*The AUCTIONEER and SOLICITOR busy themselves. The room begins to empty.*

MRS. H. Smalley? Smalley? *Is* that the Duke's agent? Jack!

HILLCRIST. [*Coming out of a sort of coma, after the excitement he has been going through*] What! What!

JILL. Oh, Dodo! How splendidly you stuck it!

HILLCRIST. Phew! What a squeak! I was clean out of my depth. A mercy the Duke chipped in again.

MRS. H. [*Looking at ROLF and CHLOE, who are standing up as if about to go*] Take care; they can hear you. Find Dawker, Jack.

> [*Below, the AUCTIONEER and SOLICITOR take up their papers, and move out Left.*

> [*HILLCRIST stretches himself, standing up, as if to throw off the strain. The door behind is opened, and HORN-BLOWER appears.*

HORNBLOWER. Ye ran me up a pretty price. Ye bid very pluckily, Hillcrist. But ye didn't quite get my measure.

HILLCRIST. Oh! It was *my* nine thousand the Duke capped. Thank God, the Centry's gone to a gentleman!

HORNBLOWER. The Duke? [*He laughs.*] No, the Centry's not gone to a gentleman, nor to a fool. It's gone to me.

HILLCRIST. What!

HORNBLOWER. I'm sorry for ye; ye're not fit to manage these things. Well, it's a monstrous price, and I've had to pay it because of your obstinacy. I shan't forget that when I come to build.

HILLCRIST. D'you mean to say that bid was for you?

HORNBLOWER. Of course I do. I told ye I was a bad man to be up against. Perhaps ye'll believe me now.

HILLCRIST. A dastardly trick!

HORNBLOWER. [*With venom*] What did ye call it—a skin game? Remember we're playin' a skin game, Hillcrist.

HILLCRIST. [*Clenching his fists*] If we were younger men——

HORNBLOWER. Ay! 'Twouldn't look pretty for us to be at fisticuffs. We'll leave the fightin' to the young ones. [*He glances at* ROLF *and* JILL; *suddenly throwing out his finger at* ROLF.] No makin' up to that young woman! I've watched ye. And as for you, missy, you leave my boy alone.

JILL. [*With suppressed passion*] Dodo, may I spit in his eye or something?

HILLCRIST. Sit down.

[JILL *sits down. He stands between her and* HORN-BLOWER.

You've won this round, sir, by a foul blow. We shall see whether you can take any advantage of it. I believe the law can stop you ruining my property.

HORNBLOWER. Make your mind easy; it can't. I've got ye in a noose, and I'm goin' to hang ye.

MRS. H. [*Suddenly*] Mr. Hornblower, as you fight foul—so shall we.

HILLCRIST. Amy!

MRS. H. [*Paying no attention*] And it will not be foul play towards you and yours. You are outside the pale.

HORNBLOWER. That's just where I am, outside *your* pale all round ye. Ye're not long for Deepwater, ma'am. Make you dispositions to go; ye'll be out in six months, I prophesy. And good riddance to the neighbourhood.

[*They are all down on the level now.*

CHLOE. [*Suddenly coming closer to* MRS. HILLCRIST] Here are your salts, thank you. Father, can't you——?

HORNBLOWER. [*Surprised*] Can't I what!

CHLOE. Can't you come to an arrangement?

MRS. H. Just so, Mr. Hornblower. Can't you?

HORNBLOWER. [*Looking from one to the other*] As we're speakin' out, ma'am, it's your behaviour to my daughter-in-law—who's as good as you—and better, to my thinking—that's more than half the reason why I've bought this property. Ye've fair got my dander up. Now it's no use to bandy words. It's very forgivin' of ye, Chloe, but come along!

MRS. H. Quite seriously, Mr. Hornblower, you had better come to an arrangement.

HORNBLOWER. Mrs. Hillcrist, ladies should keep to their own business.

MRS. H. I will.

HILLCRIST. Amy, do leave it to us men. You, young man [*he speaks to* ROLF], do you support your father's trick this afternoon?

[JILL *looks round at* ROLF, *who tries to speak, when* HORNBLOWER *breaks in.*

HORNBLOWER. *My* trick? And what d'ye call it, to try and put me own son against me?

JILL. [*To* ROLF] Well?

ROLF. I don't, but——

HORNBLOWER. Trick? Ye young cub, be quiet. Mr. Hillcrist had an agent bid for him—I had an agent bid for me. Only his agent bid at the beginnin', an' mine bid at the end. What's the trick in that? [*He laughs.*

HILLCRIST. Hopeless; we're in different worlds.

HORNBLOWER. I wish to God we were! Come you, Chloe. And you, Rolf, you follow. In six months I'll have those chimneys up, and me lorries runnin' round ye.

MRS. H. Mr. Hornblower, if you build——

HORNBLOWER. [*Looking at* MRS. HILLCRIST] Ye know—it's laughable. Ye make me pay nine thousand five hundred for a bit o' land not worth four, and ye think I'm not to get back on ye. I'm goin' on with as little consideration as if ye were a family of blackbeetles. Good afternoon!

ROLF. Father!

JILL. Oh, Dodo! He's obscene.

HILLCRIST. Mr. Hornblower, my compliments.

[HORNBLOWER, *with a stare at* HILLCRIST'S *half-smiling face, takes* CHLOE'S *arm, and half drags her towards the door on the Left. But there, in the opened doorway, are standing* DAWKER *and a* STRANGER. *They move just out of the way of the exit, looking at* CHLOE, *who sways and very nearly falls.*

HORNBLOWER. Why! Chloe! What's the matter?

CHLOE. I don't know; I'm not well to-day.

[*She pulls herself together with a great effort.*

MRS. H. [*Who has exchanged a nod with* DAWKER *and the* STRANGER] Mr. Hornblower, you build at your peril. I warn you.

HORNBLOWER. [*Turning round to speak*] Ye think yourself very cool and very smart. But I doubt this is the first time ye've been up against realities. Now, I've been up against them all my life. Don't talk to me, ma'am, about peril and that sort of nonsense; it makes no impression. Your husband called me pachydermatous. I don't know Greek, and Latin, and all that, but I've looked it out in the dictionary, and I find it means thick-skinned. And I'm none the worse for that when I have to deal with folk like you. Good afternoon.

[*He draws* CHLOE *forward, and they pass through the door followed quickly by* ROLF.

MRS. H. Thank you, Dawker.

[*She moves up to* DAWKER *and the* STRANGER, *Left, and they talk.*

JILL. Dodo! It's awful!

HILLCRIST. Well, there's nothing for it now but to smile and pay up. Poor old home! It shall be his wash-pot. Over the Centry will he cast his shoe. By Gad, Jill, I could cry!

JILL. [*Pointing*] Look! Chloe's sitting down. She nearly fainted just now. It's something to do with Dawker, Dodo, and that man with him. Look at mother! Ask them?

HILLCRIST. Dawker!

[DAWKER *comes to him, followed by* MRS. HILLCRIST.]
What's the mystery about young Mrs. Hornblower?

DAWKER. No mystery.

HILLCRIST. Well, what is it?

MRS. H. You'd better not ask.

HILLCRIST. I wish to know.

MRS. H. Jill, go out and wait for us.

JILL. Nonsense, mother.

MRS. H. It's not for a girl to hear.

JILL. Bosh! I read the papers every day.

DAWKER. It's nothin' worse than you get there, anyway.

MRS. H. Do you wish your daughter——

JILL. It's ridiculous, Dodo; you'd think I was mother at my age.

MRS. H. I was not so proud of my knowledge.

JILL. No, but you had it, dear.

HILLCRIST. What is it—what is it? Come over here, Dawker.

[DAWKER *goes to him, Right, and speaks in a low voice.*]
What! [*Again* DAWKER *speaks in a low voice.*]
Good God!

MRS. H. Exactly!

JILL. Poor thing—whatever it is!

MRS. H. Poor thing?

JILL. What went before, mother?

MRS. H. It's what's coming after that matters, luckily.

HILLCRIST. How do you know this?

DAWKER. My friend here [*He points to the* STRANGER] was one of the agents.

HILLCRIST. It's shocking. I'm sorry I heard it.

MRS. H. I told you not to.

HILLCRIST. Ask your friend to come here.

[DAWKER *beckons, and the* STRANGER *joins the group.*]
Are you sure of what you've said, sir?

STRANGER. Perfectly. I remember her quite well; her name then was——

HILLCRIST. I don't want to know, thank you. I'm truly sorry. I wouldn't wish the knowledge of that about his womenfolk to my worst enemy. This mustn't be spoken of.

[JILL *hugs his arm.*

MRS. H. It will not be if Mr. Hornblower is wise. If he is not wise, it must be spoken of.

HILLCRIST. I say no, Amy. I won't have it. It's a dirty weapon. Who touches pitch shall be defiled.

MRS. H. Well, what weapons does he use against us? Don't be quixotic. For all we can tell, they know it quite well already, and if they don't they ought to. Anyway, to know this is our salvation, and we must use it.

JILL. [*Sotto voce*] Pitch! Dodo! Pitch!

DAWKER. The threat's enough! J.P.—Chapel—Future member for the constituency——

HILLCRIST. [*A little more doubtfully*] To use a piece of knowledge about a woman—it's repugnant. I—I won't do it.

MRS. H. If you had a son tricked into marrying such a woman, would you wish to remain ignorant of it?

HILLCRIST. [*Struck*] I don't know—I don't know.

MRS. H. At least you'd like to be in a position to help him, if you thought it necessary?

HILLCRIST. Well—that—perhaps.

MRS. H. Then you agree that Mr. Hornblower at least should be told. What he does with the knowledge is not our affair.

HILLCRIST. [*Half to the* STRANGER *and half to* DAWKER] Do you realize that an imputation of that kind may be ground for a criminal libel action?

STRANGER. Quite. But there's no shadow of doubt; not the faintest. You saw her just now?

HILLCRIST. I did. [*Revolting again.*] No; I don't like it.

[DAWKER *has drawn the* STRANGER *a step or two away,
and they talk together.*

MRS. H. [*In a low voice*] And the ruin of our home?
You're betraying your fathers, Jack.

HILLCRIST. I can't bear bringing a woman into it.

MRS. H. We don't. If anyone brings her in, it will be
Hornblower himself.

HILLCRIST. We use her secret as a lever.

MRS. H. I tell you quite plainly: I will only consent to
holding my tongue about her, if you agree to Hornblower
being told. It's a scandal to have a woman like that in the
neighbourhood.

JILL. Mother means that, father.

HILLCRIST. Jill, keep quiet. This is a very bitter position.
I can't tell what to do.

MRS. H. You must use this knowledge. You owe it to
me—to us all. You'll see that when you've thought it over.

JILL. [*Softly*] Pitch, Dodo, pitch!

MRS. H. [*Furiously*] Jill, be quiet!

HILLCRIST. I was brought up never to hurt a woman. I
can't do it, Amy—I can't do it. I should never feel like a
gentleman again.

MRS. H. [*Coldly*] Oh! Very well.

HILLCRIST. What d'you mean by that?

MRS. H. I shall use the knowledge in my own way.

HILLCRIST. [*Staring at her*] You would—against my
wishes?

MRS. H. I consider it my duty.

HILLCRIST. If I agree to Hornblower being told——

MRS. H. That's all I want.

HILLCRIST. It's the utmost I'll consent to, Amy; and don't
let's have any humbug about its being morally necessary.
We do it to save our skins.

MRS. H. I don't know what you mean by humbug?

JILL. He means humbug, mother.

HILLCRIST. It must stop at old Hornblower. Do you quite understand?

MRS. H. Quite.

JILL. Will it stop?

MRS. H. Jill, if you can't keep your impertinence to yourself——

HILLCRIST. Jill, come with me.

[*He turns towards door, Back.*

JILL. I'm sorry, mother. Only it *is* a skin game, isn't it?

MRS. H. You pride yourself on plain speech, Jill. I pride myself on plain thought. You will thank me afterwards that I can see realities. I know we are better people than these Hornblowers. Here we are going to stay, and they—are not.

JILL. [*Looking at her with a sort of unwilling admiration*] Mother, you're wonderful!

HILLCRIST. Jill!

JILL. Coming, Dodo.

[*She turns and runs to the door. They go out. MRS. HILL-
CRIST, with a long sigh, draws herself up, fine and proud.*

MRS. H. Dawker!   [*He comes to her.*] I shall send him a note to-night, and word it so that he will be bound to come and see us to-morrow morning. Will you be in the study just before eleven o'clock, with this gentleman?

DAWKER. [*Nodding*] We're going to wire for his partner. I'll bring him too. Can't make too sure.

[*She goes firmly up the steps and out.*

DAWKER. [*To the* STRANGER, *with a wink*] The Squire's squeamish—too much of a gentleman. But he don't count. The grey mare's all right. You wire to Henry. I'm off to our solicitors. We'll make that old rhinoceros sell us back the Centry at a decent price. These Hornblowers—[*Laying his finger on his nose.*] We've got 'em!

The curtain falls.

SCENE II

CHLOE's *boudoir at half-past seven the same evening. A pretty room. No pictures on the walls, but two mirrors. A screen and a luxurious couch on the fireplace side, stage Left. A door rather Right of Centre Back, opening inwards. A French window, Right forward. A writing table, Right Back. Electric light burning.*

CHLOE, *in a tea-gown, is standing by the forward end of the sofa, very still, and very pale. Her lips are parted, and her large eyes stare straight before them as if seeing ghosts. The door is opened noiselessly and a* WOMAN'S *face is seen. It peers at* CHLOE, *vanishes, and the door is closed.* CHLOE *raises her hands, covers her eyes with them, drops them with a quick gesture, and looks round her. A knock. With a swift movement she slides on to the sofa, and lies prostrate, with eyes closed.*

CHLOE. [*Feebly*] Come in!

[*Her* MAID *enters; a trim, contained figure of uncertain years, in a black dress, with the face which was peering in.*]

Yes, Anna?

ANNA. Aren't you going in to dinner, ma'am?

CHLOE. [*With closed eyes*] No.

ANNA. Will you take anything here, ma'am?

CHLOE. I'd like a biscuit and a glass of champagne.

[*The* MAID, *who is standing between sofa and door, smiles.* CHLOE, *with a swift look, catches the smile.*]

Why do you smile?

ANNA. Was I, ma'am?

CHLOE. You know you were. [*Fiercely*]. Are you paid to smile at me?

ANNA. [*Immovable*] No, ma'am. Would you like some eau-de-Cologne on your forehead?

CHLOE. Yes.—No.—What's the good? [*Clasping her forehead.*] My headache won't go.

ANNA. To keep lying down's the best thing for it.

CHLOE. I have been—hours.

ANNA. [*With a smile*] Yes, ma'am.

CHLOE. [*Gathering herself up on the sofa*] Anna! Why do you do it?

ANNA. Do what, ma'am?

CHLOE. Spy on me.

ANNA. I—never! I——!

CHLOE. To spy! You're a fool, too. What is there to spy on?

ANNA. Nothing, ma'am. Of course, if you're not satisfied with me, I must give notice. Only—if I were spying, I should expect to have notice given me. I've been accustomed to ladies who wouldn't stand such a thing for a minute.

CHLOE. [*Intently*] Well, you'll take a month's wages and go to-morrow. And that's all, now.

> [ANNA *inclines her head and goes out.*
> [CHLOE, *with a sort of moan, turns over and buries her face in the cushion.*

CHLOE. [*Sitting up*] If I could see that man—if only—or Dawker——

> [*She springs up and goes to the door, but hesitates, and comes back to the head of the sofa, as* ROLF *comes in. During this scene the door is again opened stealthily, an inch or two.*

ROLF. How's the head?

CHLOE. Beastly, thanks. I'm not going in to dinner.

ROLF. Is there anything I can do for you?

CHLOE. No, dear boy. [*Suddenly looking at him.*] You don't want this quarrel with the Hillcrists to go on, do you, Rolf?

ROLF. No; I hate it.

CHLOE. Well, I think I *might* be able to stop it. Will you slip round to Dawker's—it's not five minutes—and ask him to come and see me.

ROLF. Father and Charlie wouldn't——

CHLOE. I know. But if he comes to the window here while you're at dinner, I'll let him in, and out, and nobody'd know.

ROLF. [*Astonished*] Yes, but what—I mean how——

CHLOE. Don't ask me. It's worth the shot—that's all. [*Looking at her wrist-watch.*] To this window at eight o'clock exactly. First long window on the terrace, tell him.

ROLF. It's nothing Charlie would mind?

CHLOE. No; only I can't tell him—he and father are so mad about it all.

ROLF. If there's a real chance——

CHLOE. [*Going to the window and opening it*] This way, Rolf. If you don't come back I shall know he's coming. Put your watch by mine. [*Looking at his watch.*] It's a minute fast, see!

ROLF. Look here, Chloe——

CHLOE. Don't wait; go on.

> [*She almost pushes him out through the window, closes it after him, draws the curtains again, stands a minute, thinking hard; goes to the bell and rings it; then, crossing to the writing-table, Right Back, she takes out a chemist's prescription.* [ANNA *comes in.*

CHLOE. I don't want that champagne. Take this to the chemist and get him to make up some of these cachets quick, and bring them back yourself.

ANNA. Yes, ma'am; but you have some.

CHLOE. They're too old; I've taken two—the strength's out of them. Quick, please; I can't stand this head.

ANNA. [*Taking the prescription—with her smile*] Yes, ma'am. It'll take some time—you don't want me?

CHLOE. No; I want the cachets. [ANNA *goes out.*

[CHLOE *looks at her wrist-watch, goes to the writing-table, which is old-fashioned, with a secret drawer, looks round her, dives at the secret drawer, takes out a roll of notes and a tissue paper parcel. She counts the notes:* "Three hundred." *Slips them into her breast and unwraps the little parcel. It contains pearls. She slips them too into her dress, looks round startled, replaces the drawer, and regains her place on the sofa, lying prostrate as the door opens, and* HORNBLOWER *comes in. She does not open her eyes, and he stands looking at her a moment before speaking.*

HORNBLOWER. [*Almost softly*] How are ye feelin', Chloe?

CHLOE. Awful head!

HORNBLOWER. Can ye attend a moment? I've had a note from that woman.   [CHLOE *sits up.*

HORNBLOWER. [*Reading*] "I have something of the utmost importance to tell you in regard to your daughter-in-law. I shall be waiting to see you at eleven o'clock to-morrow morning. The matter is so utterly vital to the happiness of all your family, that I cannot imagine you will fail to come." Now, what's the meaning of it? Is it sheer impudence, or lunacy, or what?

CHLOE. I don't know.

HORNBLOWER. [*Not unkindly*] Chloe, if there's anything— ye'd better tell me. Forewarned's forearmed.

CHLOE. There's nothing; unless it's—[*With a quick look at him.*]—Unless it's that my father was a—a bankrupt.

HORNBLOWER. Hech! Many a man's been that. Ye've never told us much about your family.

CHLOE. I wasn't very proud of him.

HORNBLOWER. Well, ye're not responsible for your father. If that's all, it's a relief. The bitter snobs! I'll remember it in the account I've got with them.

CHLOE. Father, don't say anything to Charlie; it'll only worry him for nothing.

HORNBLOWER. Na, no, I'll not. If *I* went bankrupt, it'd upset Chearlie, I've not a doubt. [*He laughs. Looking at her shrewdly.*] There's nothing else, before I answer her? [CHLOE *shakes her head.*] Ye're sure?

CHLOE. [*With an effort*] She may invent things, of course.

HORNBLOWER. [*Lost in his feud feeling*] Ah! but there's such a thing as the laws o' slander. If they play pranks, I'll have them up for it.

CHLOE. [*Timidly*] Couldn't you stop this quarrel, father? You said it was on my account. But *I* don't want to know them. And they do love their old home. I like the girl. You don't really need to build just there, do you? Couldn't you stop it? Do!

HORNBLOWER. Stop it? Now I've bought? Na, no! The snobs defied me, and I'm going to show them. I hate the lot of them, and I hate that little Dawker worst of all.

CHLOE. He's only their agent.

HORNBLOWER. He's a part of the whole dog-in-the-manger system that stands in my way. Ye're a woman, and ye don't understand these things. Ye wouldn't believe the struggle I've had to make my money and get my position. These country folk talk soft sawder, but to get anything from them's like gettin' butter out of a dog's mouth. If they could drive me out of here by fair means or foul, would they hesitate a moment? Not they! See what they've made me pay; and look at this letter. Selfish, mean lot o' hypocrites!

CHLOE. But they didn't begin the quarrel.

HORNBLOWER. Not openly; but underneath they did— that's their way. They began it by thwartin' me here and there and everywhere, just because I've come into me own a bit later than they did. I gave 'em their chance, and they wouldn't take it. Well, I'll show 'em what a man like me can do when he sets his mind to it. I'll not leave much skin on them.

[*In the intensity of his feeling he has lost sight of her face,
    alive with a sort of agony of doubt, whether to plead
    with him further, or what to do.   Then, with a swift
    glance at her wrist-watch, she falls back on the sofa and
    closes her eyes.*]

It'll give me a power of enjoyment seein' me chimneys go up
in front of their windies.   That was a bonnie thought—that
last bid o' mine.   He'd got that roused up, I believe he never
would a' stopped.   [*Looking at her.*] I forgot your head.
Well, well, ye'll be best lyin' quiet.   [*The gong sounds.*
Shall we send ye something in from dinner?

CHLOE.   No; I'll try to sleep.   Please tell them I don't want
to be disturbed.

HORNBLOWER.   All right.   I'll just answer this note.

[*He sits down at her writing-table.*

[CHLOE *starts up from the sofa feverishly, looking at her
    watch, at the window, at her watch; then softly
    crosses to the window and opens it.*

HORNBLOWER.   [*Finishing*] Listen!   [*He turns round towards
the sofa.*] Hallo!   Where are ye?

CHLOE.   [*At the window*] It's so hot.

HORNBLOWER.   Here's what I've said :

> "MADAM,—You can tell me nothing of my daughter-
>   in-law which can affect the happiness of my
>   family.   I regard your note as an impertinence,
>   and I shall not be with you at eleven o'clock
>   to-morrow morning.
>
> > "Yours truly——"

CHLOE.   [*With a suffering movement of her head*] Oh!—
Well!——   [*The gong is touched a second time.*

HORNBLOWER.   [*Crossing to the door*] Lie ye down, and get a
sleep.   I'll tell them not to disturb ye; and I hope ye'll be all
right to-morrow.   Good-night, Chloe.

CHLOE.   Good-night.   [*He goes out.*

[*After a feverish turn or two,* CHLOE *returns to the open
window and waits there, half screened by the curtains.
The door is opened inch by inch, and* ANNA'S *head
peers round. Seeing where* CHLOE *is, she slips in
and passes behind the screen, Left. Suddenly* CHLOE
backs in from the window.

CHLOE. [*In a low voice*] Come in. [*She darts to the door
and locks it.*

[DAWKER *has come in through the window and stands
regarding her with a half smile.*

DAWKER. Well, young woman, what do you want of me?
[*In the presence of this man of her own class, there comes
a distinct change in* CHLOE'S *voice and manner ; a
sort of frank commonness, adapted to the man she is
dealing with, but she keeps her voice low.*

CHLOE. You're making a mistake, you know.

DAWKER. [*With a broad grin*] No. I've got a memory for
faces.

CHLOE. I say you are.

DAWKER. [*Turning to go*] If that's all, you needn't 'ave
troubled me to come.

CHLOE. No. Don't go! [*With a faint smile.*] You *are*
playing a game with me. Aren't you ashamed? What harm
have I done you? Do you call this cricket?

DAWKER. No, my girl—business.

CHLOE. [*Bitterly*] What have I to do with this quarrel?
I couldn't help their falling out.

DAWKER. That's your misfortune.

CHLOE. [*Clasping her hands*] You're a cruel fellow if you
can spoil a woman's life who never did you an ounce of
harm.

DAWKER. So they *don't* know about you. That's all right.
Now, look here, I serve my employer. But I'm flesh and
blood too, and I always give as good as I get. I hate this
family of yours. There's no name too bad for 'em to call me

this last month, and no looks too black to give me.   I tell you frankly, I hate 'em.

CHLOE. There's good in them same as in you.

DAWKER. [*With a grin*] There's no good Hornblower but a dead Hornblower.

CHLOE. But—but I'm *not* one.

DAWKER. You'll be the mother of some, I shouldn't wonder.

CHLOE. [*Stretching out her hand—pathetically*] Oh! leave me alone, do! I'm happy here. Be a sport! Be a sport!

DAWKER. [*Disconcerted for a second*] You can't get at me, so don't try it on.

CHLOE. I had such a bad time in old days.

> [DAWKER *shakes his head; his grin has disappeared and his face is like wood.*

CHLOE. [*Panting*] Ah! do! You might! You've been fond of some woman, I suppose. Think of her!

DAWKER. [*Decisively*] It won't do, Mrs. Chloe. You're a pawn in the game, and I'm going to use you.

CHLOE. [*Despairingly*] What is it to you? [*With a sudden touch of the tigress.*] Look here! Don't you make an enemy of me. I haven't dragged through hell for nothing. Women like me can bite, I tell you.

DAWKER. That's better. I'd rather have a woman threaten than whine, any day. Threaten away! You'll let 'em know that you met me in the Promenade one night. Of course you'll let 'em know that, won't you?—or that——

CHLOE. Be quiet! Oh! Be quiet! [*Taking from her bosom the notes and the pearls.*] Look! There's my savings— there's all I've got! The pearls'll fetch nearly a thousand. [*Holding it out to him.*] Take it, and drop me out—won't you? Won't you?

DAWKER. [*Passing his tongue over his lips—with a hard little laugh*] You mistake your man, missis. I'm a plain dog, if you like, but I'm faithful, and I hold fast. Don't try those games on me.

CHLOE. [*Losing·control*] You're a beast!—a beast! cruel, cowardly beast! And how dare you bribe that woman here to spy on me? Oh! yes, you do; you know you do. If you drove me mad, you wouldn't care. You beast!

DAWKER. Now, don't carry on! That won't help you.

CHLOE. What d'you call it—to dog a woman down like this, just because you happen to have a quarrel with a man?

DAWKER. Who made the quarrel? Not me, missis. *You* ought to know that in a row it's the weak and helpless—we won't say the innocent—that get it in the neck. That can't be helped.

CHLOE. [*Regarding him intently*] I hope your mother or your sister, if you've got any, may go through what I'm going through ever since you got on my track. I hope they'll know what fear means. I hope they'll love and find out that it's hanging on a thread, and—and—— Oh! you coward, you persecuting coward! Call yourself a man!

DAWKER. [*With his grin*] Ah! You look quite pretty like that. By George! you're a handsome woman when you're roused.

> [CHLOE'S *passion fades out as quickly as it blazed up. She sinks down on the sofa, shudders, looks here and there, and then for a moment up at him.*

CHLOE. Is there *anything* you'll take, not to spoil my life? [*Clasping her hands on her breast; under her breath.*] Me?

DAWKER. [*Wiping his brow*] By God! That's an offer. [*He recoils towards the window.*] You—you touched me there. Look here! I've got to use you and I'm going to use you, but I'll do my best to let you down as easy as I can. No, I don't want anything you can give me—that is—— [*He wipes his brow again.*] I'd like it—but I won't take it.

> [CHLOE *buries her face in her hands.*]

There! Keep your pecker up; don't cry. Good-night!

[*He goes through the window.*

CHLOE. [*Springing up*] Ugh! Rat in a trap! Rat——!

[*She stands listening; flies to the door, unlocks it, and, going back to the sofa, lies down and closes her eyes. CHARLES comes in very quietly and stands over her, looking to see if she is asleep. She opens her eyes.*

CHARLES. Well, Clo! Had a sleep, old girl?

CHLOE. Ye—es.

CHARLES. [*Sitting on the arm of the sofa and caressing her*] Feel better, dear?

CHLOE. Yes, better, Charlie.

CHARLES. That's right. Would you like some soup?

CHLOE. [*With a shudder*] No.

CHARLES. I say—what gives you these heads? You've been very on and off all this last month.

CHLOE. I don't know. Except that—except that I *am* going to have a child, Charlie.

CHARLES. After all! By Jove! Sure?

CHLOE. [*Nodding*] Are you glad?

CHARLES. Well—I suppose I am. The guv'nor will be mighty pleased, anyway.

CHLOE. Don't tell him—yet.

CHARLES. All right! [*Bending over and drawing her to him.*] My poor girl, I'm so sorry you're seedy. Give us a kiss.

[CHLOE *puts up her face and kisses him passionately.*] I say, you're like fire. You're not feverish?

CHLOE. [*With a laugh*] It's a wonder if I'm not. Charlie, are you happy with me?

CHARLES. What do you think?

CHLOE. [*Leaning against him*] You wouldn't easily believe things against me, would you?

CHARLES. What! Thinking of those Hillcrists? What the hell that woman means by her attitude towards you——

When I saw her there to-day, I had all my work cut out not to go up and give her a bit of my mind.

CHLOE. [*Watching him stealthily*] It's not good for me, now I'm like this. It's upsetting me, Charlie.

CHARLES. Yes; and we won't forget. We'll make 'em pay for it.

CHLOE. It's wretched in a little place like this. I say, must you go on spoiling their home!

CHARLES. The woman cuts you and insults you. That's enough for me.

CHLOE. [*Timidly*] Let her. *I* don't care; I can't bear feeling enemies about, Charlie, I—get nervous—I——

CHARLES. My dear girl! What is it?

[*He looks at her intently.*

CHLOE. I suppose it's—being like this. [*Suddenly.*] But, Charlie, do stop it for my sake. Do, do!

CHARLES. [*Patting her arm*] Come, come; I say Chloe! You're making mountains. See things in proportion. Father's paid nine thousand five hundred to get the better of those people, and you want him to chuck it away to save a woman who's insulted you. That's not sense, and it's not business. Have some pride.

CHLOE. [*Breathless*] I've got no pride, Charlie. I want to be quiet—that's all.

CHARLES. Well, if the row gets on your nerves, I can take you to the sea. But you ought to enjoy a fight with people like that.

CHLOE. [*With calculated bitterness*] No, it's nothing, of course—what *I* want.

CHARLES. Hallo! Hallo! You *are* on the jump!

CHLOE. If you want me to be a good wife to you, make father stop it.

CHARLES. [*Standing up*] Now, look here, Chloe, what's behind this?

CHLOE. [*Faintly*] Behind?

G

CHARLES. You're carrying on as if—as if you were really scared! We've *got* these people. We'll have them out of Deepwater in six months. It's absolute ruination to their beastly old house; we'll put the chimneys on the very edge, not three hundred yards off, and our smoke'll be drifting over them half the time. You won't have this confounded stuck-up woman here much longer. And then we can really go ahead and take our proper place. So long as she's here, we shall never do that. We've only to drive on now as fast as we can.

CHLOE. [*With a gesture*] I see.

CHARLES. [*Again looking at her*] If you go on like this, you know, I shall begin to think there's something you——

CHLOE. [*Softly*] Charlie!   [*He comes to her.*] Love me!

CHARLES. [*Embracing her*] There, old girl! I know women are funny at these times. You want a good night, that's all.

CHLOE. You haven't finished dinner, have you? Go back, and I'll go to bed quite soon. Charlie, don't stop loving me.

CHARLES. Stop? Not much.

> [*While he is again embracing her,* ANNA *steals from behind the screen to the door, opens it noiselessly, and passes through, but it clicks as she shuts it.*

CHLOE. [*Starting violently*] Oh—h!

CHARLES. What is it? What is it? You are nervy, my dear.

CHLOE. [*Looking round with a little laugh*] I don't know. Go on, Charlie. I'll be all right when this head's gone.

CHARLES. [*Stroking her forehead and looking at her doubtfully*] You go to bed; I won't be late coming up.

> [*He turns and goes, blowing a kiss from the doorway. When he is gone,* CHLOE *gets up and stands in precisely the attitude in which she stood at the beginning of the Act, thinking, and thinking. And the door is opened, and the face of the* MAID *peers round at her.*

The curtain falls.

ACT III

SCENE I

MORNING

HILLCRIST'S *study next morning.*

[JILL, *coming from Left, looks in at the open French window.*

JILL. [*Speaking to* ROLF, *invisible*] Come in here. There's no one. [*She goes in.* ROLF *joins her, coming from the garden.*

ROLF. Jill, I just wanted to say—Need we? [JILL *nods.*] Seeing you yesterday—it did seem rotten.

JILL. *We* didn't begin it.

ROLF. No; but you don't understand. If you'd made yourself, as father has——

JILL. I hope I should be sorry.

ROLF. [*Reproachfully*] That isn't like you. Really he can't help thinking he's a public benefactor.

JILL. And we can't help thinking he's a pig. Sorry!

ROLF. If the survival of the fittest is right——

JILL. He may be fitter, but he's not going to survive.

ROLF. [*Distracted*] It looks like it though.

JILL. Is that all you came to say?

ROLF. No. Suppose we joined, couldn't we stop it?

JILL. I don't feel like joining.

ROLF. We *did* shake hands.

JILL. One can't fight and not grow bitter.

ROLF. *I* don't feel bitter.

JILL. Wait; you'll feel it soon enough.

ROLF. Why? [*Attentively.*] About Chloe? I do think your mother's manner to her is——

JILL. Well?

ROLF. Snobbish.   [JILL *laughs*.]
She may not be your class; and that's just why it's snobbish.

JILL. I think you'd better shut up.

ROLF. What my father said was true; your mother's rude-
ness to her that day she came here, has made both him and
Charlie ever so much more bitter.

[JILL *whistles the Habanera from* " *Carmen*."]

[*Staring at her, rather angrily*] Is it a whistling matter?

JILL. No.

ROLF. I suppose you want me to go?

JILL. Yes.

ROLF. All right. Aren't we ever going to be friends
again?

JILL. [*Looking steadily at him*] I don't expect so.

ROLF. That's very—horrible.

JILL. Lots of horrible things in the world.

ROLF. It's our business to make them fewer, Jill.

JILL. [*Fiercely*] Don't be moral.

ROLF. [*Hurt*] That's the last thing I want to be. I only
want to be friendly.

JILL. Better be real first.

ROLF. From the big point of view——

JILL. There isn't any. We're all out for our own. And
why not?

ROLF. By jove, you have got——

JILL. Cynical? Your father's motto—" Every man for
himself." That's the winner—hands down. Good-bye!

ROLF. Jill! Jill!

JILL. [*Putting her hands behind her back, hums*] :

> " If auld acquaintance be forgot
>   And days of auld lang syne—— "

ROLF. Don't!

[*With a pained gesture he goes out towards Left, through the
French window.*

[JILL, *who has broken off the song, stands with her hands clenched and her lips quivering.*]

[FELLOWS *enters Left.*

FELLOWS. Mr. Dawker, Miss, and two gentlemen.

JILL. Let the three gentlemen in, and me out.

[*She passes him and goes out Left.*

[*And immediately* DAWKER *and the* TWO STRANGERS *come in.*

FELLOWS. I'll inform Mrs. Hillcrist, sir. The Squire is on his rounds.   [*He goes out Left.*

[*The* THREE MEN *gather in a discreet knot at the big bureau, having glanced at the two doors and the open French window.*

DAWKER. Now this may come into Court, you know. If there's a screw loose anywhere, better mention it. [*To* SECOND STRANGER.] You knew her personally?

SECOND S. What do you think? I don't take girls on trust for that sort of job. She came to us highly recommended, too; and did her work very well. It was a double stunt—to make sure—wasn't it, George?

FIRST S. Yes; we paid her for the two visits.

SECOND S. I should know her in a minute; striking-looking girl; had something in her face. Daresay she'd seen hard times.

FIRST S. We don't want publicity.

DAWKER. Not likely. The threat'll do it; but the stakes are heavy—and the man's a slogger; we must be able to push it home. If you can both swear to her, it'll do the trick.

SECOND S. And about—I mean, we're losing time, you know, coming down here.

DAWKER. [*With a nod at* FIRST STRANGER] George here knows me. That'll be all right. I'll guarantee it well worth your while.

SECOND S. I don't want to do the girl harm, if she's married.

DAWKER. No, no; nobody wants to hurt *her*. We just want a cinch on this fellow till he squeals.

[*They separate a little as* MRS. HILLCRIST *enters from Right.*

DAWKER. Good morning, ma'am. My friend's partner. Hornblower coming?

MRS. H. At eleven. I had to send up a second note, Dawker.

DAWKER. Squire not in?

MRS. H. I haven't told him.

DAWKER. [*Nodding*] Our friends might go in here [*Pointing Right*] and we can use 'em as we want 'em.

MRS. H. [*To the* STRANGERS] Will you make yourselves comfortable?

[*She holds the door open, and they pass her into the room, Right.*

DAWKER. [*Showing document*] I've had this drawn and engrossed. Pretty sharp work. Conveys the Centry, *and* Longmeadow, to the Squire at four thousand five hundred. Now, ma'am, suppose Hornblower puts his hand to that, he'll have been done in the eye, and six thousand all told out o' pocket. You'll have a very nasty neighbour here.

MRS. H. But we shall still have the power to disclose that secret at any time.

DAWKER. Yeh! But things might happen here you could never bring home to him. You can't trust a man like that. He isn't goin' to forgive *me*, I know.

MRS. H. [*Regarding him keenly*] But if he signs, we couldn't honourably——

DAWKER. No, ma'am, *you* couldn't; and I'm sure *I* don't want to do that girl a hurt. I just mention it because, of course, you can't guarantee that it doesn't get out.

MRS. H. Not absolutely, I suppose.

[*A look passes between them, which neither of them has quite sanctioned.*]

There's his car.   It always seems to make more noise than any other.

DAWKER. He'll kick and flounder—but you leave him to ask what you want, ma'am; don't mention this. [*He puts the deed back into his pocket.*] The Centry's no mortal good to him if he's not going to put up works; I should say he'd be glad to save what he can.

[MRS. HILLCRIST *inclines her head.* FELLOWS *enters Left.*

FELLOWS. [*Apologetically*] Mr. Hornblower, ma'am; by appointment, he says.

MRS. H. Quite right, Fellows.

[HORNBLOWER *comes in, and* FELLOWS *goes out.*

HORNBLOWER. [*Without salutation*] I've come to ask ye point blank what ye mean by writing me these letters. [*He takes out two letters.*]   And we'll discuss it in the presence of nobody, if ye please.

MRS. H. Mr. Dawker knows all that I know, and more.

HORNBLOWER. Does he? Very well! Your second note says that my daughter-in-law has lied to me. Well, I've brought her, and what ye've got to say—if it's not just a trick to see me again—ye'll say to her face.

[*He takes a step towards the window.*

MRS. H. Mr. Hornblower, you had better decide that after hearing what it is—we shall be quite ready to repeat it in her presence; but we want to do as little harm as possible.

HORNBLOWER. [*Stopping*] Oh! ye do! Well, what lies have ye been hearin'? Or what have ye made up? You and Mr. Dawker? Of course ye know there's a law of libel and slander. I'm not the man to stop at that.

MRS. H. [*Calmly*] Are you familiar with the law of divorce, Mr. Hornblower?

HORNBLOWER. [*Taken aback*] No, I'm not.   That is——

MRS. H. Well, you know that misconduct is required. And I suppose you've heard that cases are arranged.

HORNBLOWER. I know it's all very shocking—what about it?

MRS. H. When cases are arranged, Mr. Hornblower, the man who is to be divorced often visits an hotel with a strange woman. I am extremely sorry to say that your daughter-in-law, before her marriage, was in the habit of being employed as such a woman.

HORNBLOWER. Ye dreadful creature!

DAWKER. [*Quickly*] All proved, up to the hilt!

HORNBLOWER. I don't believe a word of it. Ye're lyin' to save your skins. How dare ye tell me such monstrosities? Dawker, I'll have ye in a criminal court.

DAWKER. Rats! You saw a gent with me yesterday? Well, *he's* employed her.

HORNBLOWER. A put-up job! Conspiracy!

MRS. H. Go and get your daughter-in-law.

HORNBLOWER. [*With the first sensation of being in a net*] It's a foul shame—a lying slander!

MRS. H. If so, it's easily disproved. Go and fetch her.

HORNBLOWER. [*Seeing them unmoved*] I will. I don't believe a word of it.

MRS. H. I hope you are right.

> [HORNBLOWER *goes out by the French window.* DAWKER *slips to the door Right, opens it, and speaks to those within.* MRS. HILLCRIST *stands moistening her lips, and passing her handkerchief over them.* HORNBLOWER *returns, preceding* CHLOE, *strung up to hardness and defiance.*

HORNBLOWER. Now then, let's have this impudent story torn to rags.

CHLOE. What story?

HORNBLOWER. That you, my dear, were a woman—it's too shockin'—I don't know how to tell ye——

CHLOE. Go on!

HORNBLOWER. Were a woman that went with men, to get them their divorce.

CHLOE. Who says that?

HORNBLOWER. That lady [*sneering*] there, and her bull-terrier here.

CHLOE. [*Facing* MRS. HILLCRIST] That's a charitable thing to say, isn't it?

MRS. H. Is it true?

CHLOE. No.

HORNBLOWER. [*Furiously*] There! I'll have ye both on your knees to her!

DAWKER. [*Opening the door Right*] Come in.

> [*The* FIRST STRANGER *comes in.* CHLOE, *with a visible effort, turns to face him.*

FIRST S. How do you do, Mrs. Vane?

CHLOE. I don't know you.

FIRST S. Your memory is bad, ma'am. You knew me yesterday well enough. One day is not a long time, nor are three years.

CHLOE. Who *are* you?

FIRST S. Come, ma'am, come! The Custer case.

CHLOE. I don't know you, I say. [*To* MRS. HILLCRIST.] How can you be so vile?

FIRST S. Let me refresh your memory, ma'am. [*Producing a note-book.*] Just on three years ago: "Oct. 3. To fee and expenses Mrs. Vane with Mr. C——, Hotel Beaulieu, Twenty pounds. Oct. 10, Do., Twenty pounds." [*To* HORNBLOWER.] Would you like to glance at this book, sir? You'll see they're genuine entries.

> [HORNBLOWER *makes a motion to do so, but checks himself and looks at* CHLOE.

CHLOE. [*Hysterically*] It's all lies—lies!

FIRST S. Come, ma'am, we wish you no harm.

CHLOE. Take me away. I won't be treated like this.

MRS. H. [*In a low voice*] Confess.

CHLOE. Lies!

HORNBLOWER. Were ye ever called Vane?

CHLOE. No, never.

> [*She makes a movement towards the window, but* DAWKER *is in the way, and she halts.*]

FIRST S. [*Opening the door Right*] Henry.

> [*The* SECOND STRANGER *comes in quickly. At sight of him* CHLOE *throws up her hands, gasps, breaks down stage Left, and stands covering her face with her hands. It is so complete a confession that* HORNBLOWER *stands staggered; and, taking out a coloured handkerchief, wipes his brow.*]

DAWKER. Are you convinced?

HORNBLOWER. Take those men away.

DAWKER. If you're not satisfied, we can get other evidence; plenty.

HORNBLOWER. [*Looking at* CHLOE] That's enough.   Take them out.   Leave me alone with her.

> [DAWKER *takes them out Right*
> [MRS. HILLCRIST *passes* HORNBLOWER *and goes out at the window.* HORNBLOWER *moves down a step or two towards* CHLOE.

HORNBLOWER. My God!

CHLOE. [*With an outburst*] Don't tell Charlie! Don't tell Charlie!

HORNBLOWER. Chearlie!   So that was your manner of life!   [CHLOE *utters a moaning sound.*]
So that's what ye got out of by marryin' into my family! Shame on ye, ye Godless thing!

CHLOE. Don't tell Charlie!

HORNBLOWER. And that's all ye can say for the wreck ye've wrought.   My family, my works, my future!   How dared ye!

CHLOE. If you'd been me——!

HORNBLOWER. An' these Hillcrists.   The skin game of it!

CHLOE. [*Breathless*] Father!

HORNBLOWER. Don't call me that, woman!

CHLOE. [*Desperate*] I'm going to have a child.

HORNBLOWER. God! Ye are!

CHLOE. Your grandchild. For the sake of it, do what these people want; and don't tell anyone—— *Don't tell Charlie!*

HORNBLOWER. [*Again wiping his forehead*] A secret between us. I don't know that I can keep it. It's horrible. Poor Chearlie!

CHLOE. [*Suddenly fierce*] You must keep it, you shall! I won't have him told. Don't make me desperate! I can be—I didn't live that life for nothing.

HORNBLOWER. [*Staring at her revealed in a new light*] Ay; ye look a strange, wild woman, as I see ye. And we thought the world of ye!

CHLOE. I love Charlie; I'm faithful to him. I can't live without him. You'll never forgive me, I know; but Charlie——! [*Stretching out her hands.*

[HORNBLOWER *makes a bewildered gesture with his large hands.*

HORNBLOWER. I'm all at sea here. Go out to the car and wait for me. [CHLOE *passes him and goes out, Left.*]
[*Muttering to himself.*] So I'm down! Me enemies put their heels upon me head! Ah! but we'll see yet!

[*He goes up to the window and beckons towards the Right.*]
[MRS. HILLCRIST *comes in.*]

What d'ye want for this secret?

MRS. H. Nothing.

HORNBLOWER. Indeed! Wonderful!—the trouble ye've taken for—nothing.

MRS. H. If you harm us we shall harm you. Any use whatever of the Centry——

HORNBLOWER. For which ye made me pay nine thousand five hundred pounds.

MRS. H. We will buy it from you.

HORNBLOWER. At what price?

MRS. H. The Centry at the price Miss Mullins would have

taken at first, and Longmeadow at the price you gave us—
four thousand five hundred altogether.

HORNBLOWER. A fine price, and me six thousand out of
pocket. Na, no! I'll keep it and hold it over ye. Ye
daren't tell this secret so long as I've got it.

MRS. H. No, Mr. Hornblower. On second thoughts, you
must sell. You broke your word over the Jackmans. We
can't trust you. We would rather have our place here ruined
at once, than leave you the power to ruin it as and when you
like. You will sell us the Centry and Longmeadow now, or
you know what will happen.

HORNBLOWER. [*Writhing*] I'll not. It's blackmail.

MRS. H. Very well then! Go your own way and we'll go
ours. There is no witness to this conversation.

HORNBLOWER. [*Venomously*] By heaven, ye're a clever
woman. Will ye swear by Almighty God that you and
your family, and that agent of yours, won't breathe a word of
this shockin' thing to mortal soul?

MRS. H. Yes, if you sell.

HORNBLOWER. Where's Dawker?

MRS. H. [*Going to the door, Right*] Mr. Dawker!

[DAWKER *comes in.*

HORNBLOWER. I suppose ye've got your iniquity ready.

[DAWKER *grins and produces the document.*]
It's mighty near conspiracy, this. Have ye got a Testament?

MRS. H. My word will be enough, Mr. Hornblower.

HORNBLOWER. Ye'll pardon me—I can't make it solemn
enough for you.

MRS. H. Very well; here is a Bible.

[*She takes a small Bible from the bookshelf.*

DAWKER. [*Spreading document on bureau*] This is a short
conveyance of the Centry and Longmeadow—recites sale to
you by Miss Mullins of the first, John Hillcrist of the second,
and whereas you have agreed for the sale to said John Hillcrist,
for the sum of four thousand five hundred pounds, in con-

sideration of the said sum, receipt whereof you hereby acknowledge, you do convey all that, etc. Sign here. I'll witness.

HORNBLOWER. [*To* MRS. HILLCRIST] Take that Book in your hand, and swear first. I swear by Almighty God never to breathe a word of what I know concerning Chloe Hornblower to any living soul.

MRS. H. No, Mr. Hornblower; you will please sign first. *We* are not in the habit of breaking our words.

> [HORNBLOWER, *after a furious look at them, seizes a pen, runs his eye again over the deed, and signs,* DAWKER *witnessing.*]

To that oath, Mr. Hornblower, we shall add the words, " So long as the Hornblower family do us no harm,"

HORNBLOWER. [*With a snarl*] Take it in your hands, both of ye, and together swear.

MRS. H. [*Taking the Book*] I swear that I will breathe no word of what I know concerning Chloe Hornblower to any living soul, so long as the Hornblower family do us no harm.

DAWKER. I swear that too.

MRS. H. I engage for my husband.

HORNBLOWER. Where are those two fellows?

DAWKER. Gone. It's no business of theirs.

HORNBLOWER. It's no business of any of ye what has happened to a woman in the past. Ye know that. Good-day!

> [*He gives them a deadly look, and goes out, Left, followed by* DAWKER.

MRS. H. [*With her hand on the Deed*] Safe!

> [HILLCRIST *enters at the French window, followed by* JILL.]

[*Holding up the Deed.*] Look! He's just gone! I told you it was only necessary to use the threat. He caved in and signed this; we are sworn to say nothing. We've beaten him. [HILLCRIST *studies the Deed.*

JILL. [*Awed*] We saw Chloe in the car. How did she take it, mother?

MRS. H. Denied, then broke down when she saw our witnesses. I'm glad you were not here, Jack.

JILL. [*Suddenly*] I shall go and see her.

MRS. H. Jill, you will *not*; you don't know what she's done.

JILL. I shall. She must be in an awful state.

HILLCRIST. My dear, you can do her no good.

JILL. I think I can, Dodo.

MRS. H. You don't understand human nature. We're enemies for life with those people. You're a little donkey if you think anything else.

JILL. I'm going, all the same.

MRS. H. Jack, forbid her.

HILLCRIST. [*Lifting an eyebrow*] Jill, be reasonable.

JILL. Suppose I'd taken a knock like that, Dodo, I'd be glad of friendliness from someone.

MRS. H. You never *could* take a knock like *that*.

JILL. You don't know what you can do till you try, mother.

HILLCRIST. Let her go, Amy. I'm sorry for that young woman.

MRS. H. You'd be sorry for a man who picked your pocket, I believe.

HILLCRIST. I certainly should! Deuced little he'd get out of it, when I've paid for the Centry.

MRS. H. [*Bitterly*] Much gratitude I get for saving you both our home!

JILL. [*Disarmed*] Oh! Mother, we *are* grateful. Dodo, show your gratitude.

HILLCRIST. Well, my dear, it's an intense relief. I'm not good at showing my feelings, as you know. What d'you want me to do? Stand on one leg and crow?

JILL. *Yes*, Dodo, yes! Mother, hold him while I— [*Suddenly she stops, and all the fun goes out of her.*] No! I can't— I can't help thinking of *her*.

The curtain falls for a minute.

SCENE II

EVENING

When it rises again, the room is empty and dark, save for moonlight
coming in through the French window, which is open.

The figure of CHLOE, *in a black cloak, appears outside in the moon-*
light; she peers in, moves past, comes back, hesitatingly
enters. The cloak, fallen back, reveals a white evening
dress; and that magpie figure stands poised watchfully in the
dim light, then flaps unhappily Left and Right, as if she
could not keep still. Suddenly she stands listening.

ROLF'S VOICE. [*Outside*] Chloe! Chloe!   [*He appears.*

CHLOE. [*Going to the window*] What are you doing here?

ROLF. What are *you*? I only followed you.

CHLOE. Go away!

ROLF. What's the matter? Tell me!

CHLOE. Go away, and don't say anything. Oh! The
roses! [*She has put her nose into some roses in a bowl on a big
stand close to the window.*] Don't they smell lovely?

ROLF. What did Jill want this afternoon?

CHLOE. I'll tell you nothing. Go away!

ROLF. I don't like leaving you here in this state.

CHLOE. What state? I'm all right. Wait for me down in
the drive, if you want to.

        [ROLF *starts to go, stops, looks at her, and does go.*
        [CHLOE, *with a little moaning sound, flutters again,*
            magpie-like, up and down, then stands by the window
            listening. Voices are heard, Left. She darts out of
            the window and away to the Right, as HILLCRIST
            and JILL *come in. They have turned up the electric*
            light, and come down in front of the fireplace, where
            HILLCRIST *sits in an armchair, and* JILL *on the arm of*
            it. They are in undress evening attire.

HILLCRIST. Now, tell me.

JILL. There isn't much, Dodo. I was in an awful funk for fear I should meet any of the others, and of course I did meet Rolf, but I told him some lie, and he took me to her room—boudoir, they call it—isn't boudoir a "dug-out" word?

HILLCRIST. [*Meditatively*] The sulking room. Well?

JILL. She was sitting like this. [*She buries her chin in her hands, with her elbows on her knees.*] And she said in a sort of fierce way: "What do you want?" And I said: "I'm awfully sorry, but I thought you might like it."

HILLCRIST. Well?

JILL. She looked at me hard, and said: "I suppose you know all about it." And I said: "Only vaguely," because of course I don't. And she said: "Well, it was decent of you to come." Dodo, she looks like a lost soul. What has she done?

HILLCRIST. She committed her real crime when she married young Hornblower without telling him. She came out of a certain world to do it.

JILL. Oh! [*Staring in front of her.*] Is it very awful in that world, Dodo?

HILLCRIST. [*Uneasy*] I don't know, Jill. Some can stand it, I suppose; some can't. I don't know which sort she is.

JILL. One thing I'm sure of: she's awfully fond of Chearlie.

HILLCRIST. That's bad; that's very bad.

JILL. And she's frightened, horribly. I think she's desperate.

HILLCRIST. Women like that are pretty tough, Jill; don't judge her too much by your own feelings.

JILL. No; only—— Oh! it was beastly; and of course I dried up.

HILLCRIST. [*Feelingly*] H'm! One always does. But perhaps it was as well; you'd have been blundering in a dark passage.

JILL. I just said : " Father and I feel awfully sorry; if there's anything we can do——"

HILLCRIST. That was risky, Jill.

JILL. [Disconsolately] I had to say something. I'm glad I went, anyway. I feel more human.

HILLCRIST. We had to fight for our home. I should have felt like a traitor if I hadn't.

JILL. I'm not enjoying home to-night, Dodo.

HILLCRIST. I never could hate properly; it's a confounded nuisance.

JILL. Mother's fearfully bucked, and Dawker's simply oozing triumph. I don't trust him, Dodo; he's too—not pugilistic—the other one with a pug—nacious.

HILLCRIST. He is rather.

JILL. I'm sure he wouldn't care tuppence if Chloe committed suicide.

HILLCRIST. [Rising uneasily] Nonsense! Nonsense!

JILL. I wonder if mother would.

HILLCRIST. [Turning his face towards the window] What's that? I thought I heard—[Louder.] Is there anybody out there?

[No answer. JILL springs up and runs to the window.

JILL. You! [She dives through to the Right, and returns, holding CHLOE'S hand and drawing her forward.] Come in! It's only us! [To HILLCRIST.] Dodo!

HILLCRIST. [Flustered, but making a show of courtesy] Good evening! Won't you sit down?

JILL. Sit down; you're all shaky.

[She makes CHLOE sit down in the armchair, out of which they have risen, then locks the door, and closing the windows, draws the curtains hastily over them.

HILLCRIST. [Awkward and expectant] Can I do anything for you?

CHLOE. I couldn't bear it—he's coming to ask you——

HILLCRIST. Who?

CHLOE. My husband. [*She draws in her breath with a long shudder, then seems to seize her courage in her hands.*] I've got to be quick. He keeps on asking—he knows there's something.

HILLCRIST. Make your mind easy. We shan't tell him.

CHLOE. [*Appealing*] Oh! that's not enough. Can't you tell him something to put him back to thinking it's all right? I've done him such a wrong. I didn't realize till after—I thought meeting him was just a piece of wonderful good luck, after what I'd been through. I'm not such a bad lot—not really.   [*She stops from the over-quivering of her lips.*

[JILL, *standing beside the chair, strokes her shoulder.* HILL-CRIST *stands very still, painfully biting at a finger.*]

You see, my father went bankrupt, and I was in a shop till——

HILLCRIST. [*Soothingly, and to prevent disclosures*] Yes, yes; yes, yes.

CHLOE. I never gave a man away or did anything I was ashamed of—at least—I mean, I had to make my living in all sorts of ways, and then I met Charlie.

[*Again she stops from the quivering of her lips.*

JILL. It's all right.

CHLOE. He thought I was respectable, and that was such a relief, you can't think, so—so I let him.

JILL. Dodo! It's awful!

HILLCRIST. It is!

CHLOE. And after I married him, you see, I fell in love. If I had before, perhaps I wouldn't have dared—only, I don't know—you never know, do you? When there's a straw going, you catch at it.

JILL. Of course you do.

CHLOE. And now, you see, I'm going to have a child.

JILL. [*Aghast*] Oh! Are you?

HILLCRIST. Good God!

CHLOE. [*Dully*] I've been on hot bricks all this month, ever since—that day here. I knew it was in the wind. What gets in the wind never gets out. [*She rises and throws out her arms.*] Never! It just blows here and there, [*Desolately*] and then blows home. [*Her voice changes to resentment.*] But I've paid for being a fool—'tisn't fun that sort of life, I can tell you. I'm not ashamed and repentant, and all that. If it wasn't for him; I'm afraid he'll never forgive me; it's such a disgrace for him—and then, to have his child! Being fond of him, I feel it much worse than anything I ever felt, and that's saying a good bit. It is.

JILL. [*Energetically*] Look here! He simply mustn't find out.

CHLOE. That's it; but it's started, and he's bound to keep on because he knows there's something. A man isn't going to be satisfied when there's something he suspects about his wife. Charlie wouldn't—never. He's clever, and he's jealous; and he's coming here.

[*She stops, and looks round wildly, listening.*

JILL. Dodo, what can we say to put him clean off the scent?

HILLCRIST. Anything in reason.

CHLOE. [*Catching at this straw*] You will! You see, I don't know what I'll do. I've got soft, being looked after—he does love me. And if he throws me off, I'll go under—that's all.

HILLCRIST. Have you any suggestion?

CHLOE. [*Eagerly*] The only thing is to tell him something positive, something he'll believe, that's not *too* bad—like my having been a lady clerk with those people who came here, and having been dismissed on suspicion of taking money. I could get him to believe that wasn't true.

JILL. Yes; and it isn't—that's splendid! You'd be able to put such conviction into it. Don't you think so, Dodo?

HILLCRIST. Anything I can. I'm deeply sorry.

CHLOE. Thank you. And don't say I've been here, will you? He's very suspicious. You see, he knows that his father has re-sold that land to you; that's what he can't make out—that, and my coming here this morning; he knows something's being kept from him; and he noticed that man with Dawker yesterday. And my maid's been spying on me. It's in the air. He puts two and two together. But I've told him there's nothing he need worry about; nothing that's true.

HILLCRIST. What a coil!

CHLOE. I'm very honest and careful about money. So he won't believe that about me, and the old man wants to keep it from Charlie, I know.

HILLCRIST. That does seem the best way out.

CHLOE. [*With a touch of defiance*] I'm a true wife to him.

JILL. Of course we know that.

HILLCRIST. It's all unspeakably sad. Deception's horribly against the grain—but——

CHLOE. [*Eagerly*] When I deceived him, I'd have deceived God Himself—I was so desperate. You've never been right down in the mud. You can't understand what I've been through.

HILLCRIST. Yes, yes. I daresay I'd have done the same. I should be the last to judge——

　　　　　　　[CHLOE *covers her eyes with her hands.*]
There, there! Cheer up!　　　　[*He puts his hand on her arm.*

JILL. [*To herself*] Darling Dodo!

CHLOE. [*Starting*] There's somebody at the door. I must go; I must go.

　　　　　[*She runs to the window and slips through the curtains.*
　　　　　　　[*The handle of the door is again turned.*

JILL. [*Dismayed*] Oh! It's locked—I forgot.
　　[*She springs to the door, unlocks and opens it, while* HILL-
　　　　　CRIST *goes to the bureau and sits down.*]
It's all right, Fellows; I was only saying something rather important.

FELLOWS. [*Coming in a step or two and closing the door behind him*] Certainly, Miss. Mr. Charles 'Ornblower is in the hall. Wants to see you, sir, or Mrs. Hillcrist.

JILL. What a bore! Can you see him, Dodo?

HILLCRIST. Er—yes. I suppose so. Show him in here, Fellows.

[As FELLOWS *goes out,* JILL *runs to the window, but has no time to do more than adjust the curtains and spring over to stand by her father, before* CHARLES *comes in. Though in evening clothes, he is white and dishevelled for so spruce a young man.*

CHARLES. Is my wife here?

HILLCRIST. No, sir.

CHARLES. Has she been?

HILLCRIST. This morning, I believe, Jill?

JILL. Yes, she came this morning.

CHARLES. [*Staring at her*] I know that—*now,* I mean?

JILL. No.   [HILLCRIST *shakes his head.*

CHARLES. Tell me what was said this morning.

HILLCRIST. I was not here this morning.

CHARLES. Don't try to put me off. I know too much. [*To* JILL.] You.

JILL. Shall I, Dodo?

HILLCRIST. No; I will. Won't you sit down?

CHARLES. No. Go on.

HILLCRIST. [*Moistening his lips*] It appears, Mr. Hornblower, that my agent, Mr. Dawker——

[CHARLES, *who is breathing hard, utters a sound of anger.*]

—that my agent happens to know a firm, who in old days employed your wife. I should greatly prefer not to say any more, especially as we don't believe the story.

JILL. No; we don't.

CHARLES. Go on!

HILLCRIST. [*Getting up*] Come! If I were you, I should refuse to listen to anything against my wife.

CHARLES. Go on, I tell you.

HILLCRIST. You insist! Well, they say there was some

question about the accounts, and your wife left them under a cloud.   As I told you, we don't believe it.

CHARLES. [*Passionately*] Liars!

[*He makes a rush for the door.*

HILLCRIST. [*Starting*] What did you say?

JILL. [*Catching his arm*] Dodo! [*Sotto voce.*] We are, you know.

CHARLES. [*Turning back to them*] Why do you tell me that lie?   When I've just had the truth out of that little scoundrel! My wife's been here; she put you up to it.

[*The face of* CHLOE *is seen transfixed between the curtains, parted by her hands.*]

She—she put you up to it.   Liar that she is—a living lie.   For three years a living lie.

[HILLCRIST, *whose face alone is turned towards the curtains, sees that listening face.   His hand goes up from uncontrollable emotion.*]

And hasn't now the pluck to tell me.   I've done with her. I won't own a child by such a woman.

[*With a little sighing sound* CHLOE *drops the curtain and vanishes.*

HILLCRIST. For God's sake, man, think of what you're saying.   She's in great distress.

CHARLES. And what am I?

JILL. She loves you, you know.

CHARLES. Pretty love!   That scoundrel Dawker told me— told me—— Horrible! Horrible!

HILLCRIST. I deeply regret that our quarrel should have brought this about.

CHARLES. [*With intense bitterness*] Yes, you've smashed my life.

[*Unseen by them,* MRS. HILLCRIST *has entered and stands by the door, Left.*

MRS. H. Would you have wished to live on in ignorance?

[*They all turn to look at her.*

CHARLES. [*With a writhing movement*] I don't know. But—
you—you did it.

MRS. H. You shouldn't have attacked us.

CHARLES. What did we do to you—compared with this?

MRS. H. All you could.

HILLCRIST. Enough, enough! What can we do to help
you?

CHARLES. Tell me where my wife is.

[JILL *draws the curtains apart—the window is open—*JILL
looks out. They wait in silence.

JILL. We don't know.

CHARLES. Then she *was* here?

HILLCRIST. Yes, sir; and she heard you.

CHARLES. All the better if she did. She knows how I feel.

HILLCRIST. Brace up; be gentle with her.

CHARLES. Gentle? A woman who—who——

HILLCRIST. A most unhappy creature. Come!

CHARLES. Damn your sympathy!

[*He goes out into the moonlight, passing away Left.*

JILL. Dodo, we ought to look for her; I'm awfully
afraid.

HILLCRIST. I saw her there—listening. With child! Who
knows where things end when they once begin? To the
gravel pit, Jill; I'll go to the pond. No, we'll go together.

[*They go out.*

[MRS. HILLCRIST *comes down to the fireplace, rings the
bell and stands there, thinking.* FELLOWS *enters.*

MRS. H. I want someone to go down to Mr. Dawker's.

FELLOWS. Mr. Dawker is here, ma'am, waitin' to see you.

MRS. H. Ask him to come in. Oh! and, Fellows, you
can tell the Jackmans that they can go back to their cottage.

FELLOWS. Very good, ma'am.   [*He goes out.*

[MRS. HILLCRIST *searches at the bureau, finds and takes
out the deed.* DAWKER *comes in; he has the appearance of a man whose temper has been badly ruffled.*

MRS. H. Charles Hornblower—how did it happen?

DAWKER. He came to me. I said I knew nothing. He wouldn't take it; went for me, abused me up hill and down dale; said he knew everything, and then he began to threaten me. Well, I lost my temper, and I told him.

MRS. H. That's very serious, Dawker, after our promise. My husband is most upset.

DAWKER. [*Sullenly*] It's not my fault, ma'am; he shouldn't have threatened and goaded me on. Besides, it's got out that there's a scandal; common talk in the village—not the facts, but quite enough to cook their goose here. They'll have to go. Better have done with it, anyway, than have enemies at your door.

MRS. H. Perhaps; but—— Oh! Dawker, take charge of this. [*She hands him the deed.*] These people are desperate—and—I'm not sure of my husband when his feelings are worked on. [*The sound of a car stopping.*

DAWKER. [*At the window, looking to the Left*] Hornblower's, I think. Yes, he's getting out.

MRS. H. [*Bracing herself*] You'd better wait, then.

DAWKER. He mustn't give me any of his sauce; I've had enough.

[*The door is opened and* HORNBLOWER *enters, pressing so on the heels of* FELLOWS *that the announcement of his name is lost.*

HORNBLOWER. Give me that deed! Ye got it out of me by false pretences and treachery. Yes wore that nothing should be heard of this. Why! me own servants know!

MRS. H. That has nothing to do with us. Your son came and wrenched the knowledge out of Mr. Dawker by abuse and threats; that is all. You will kindly behave yourself here, or I shall ask that you be shown out.

HORNBLOWER. Give me that deed, I say! [*He suddenly turns on* DAWKER.] Ye little ruffian, I see it in your pocket.

[*The end indeed is projecting from* DAWKER'S *breast pocket.*

DAWKER. [*Seeing red*] Now, look 'ere, 'Ornblower, I stood a deal from your son, and I'll stand no more.

HORNBLOWER. [*To* MRS. HILLCRIST] I'll ruin your place yet! [*To* DAWKER.] Ye give me that deed, or I'll throttle you.

[*He closes on* DAWKER, *and makes a snatch at the deed.* DAWKER *springs at him, and the two stand swaying, trying for a grip at each other's throats.* MRS. HILLCRIST *tries to cross and reach the bell, but is shut off by their swaying struggle.*

[*Suddenly* ROLF *appears in the window, looks wildly at the struggle, and seizes* DAWKER'S *hands, which have reached* HORNBLOWER'S *throat.* JILL, *who is following, rushes up to him and clutches his arm.*

JILL. Rolf! All of you! Stop! Look!

[DAWKER'S *hand relaxes, and he is swung round.* HORNBLOWER *staggers and recovers himself, gasping for breath. All turn to the window, outside which in the moonlight* HILLCRIST *and* CHARLES HORNBLOWER *have* CHLOE'S *motionless body in their arms.*]

In the gravel pit. She's just breathing; that's all.

MRS. H. Bring her in. The brandy, Jill!

HORNBLOWER. No. Take her to the car. Stand back, young woman! I want no help from any of ye. Rolf—Chearlie—take her up.

[*They lift and bear her away, Left.* JILL *follows.*]

Hillcrist, ye've got me beaten and disgraced hereabouts, ye've destroyed my son's married life, and ye've killed my grandchild. I'm not staying in this cursed spot, but if ever I can do you or yours a hurt, I will.

DAWKER. [*Muttering*] That's right. Squeal and threaten. You began it.

HILLCRIST. Dawker, have the goodness! Hornblower, in

the presence of what may be death, with all my heart I'm sorry.

HORNBLOWER. Ye hypocrite!

> [*He passes them with a certain dignity, and goes out at the window, following to his car.*

> [HILLCRIST, *who has stood for a moment stock-still, goes slowly forward and sits in his swivel chair.*

MRS. H. Dawker, please tell Fellows to telephone to Dr. Robinson to go round to the Hornblowers *at once.*

> [DAWKER, *fingering the deed, and with a noise that sounds like* " The cur ! " *goes out, Left.*]

[*At the fireplace.*] Jack!   Do you blame me?

HILLCRIST. [*Motionless*] No.

MRS. H. Or Dawker?   He's done his best.

HILLCRIST. No.

MRS. H. [*Approaching*] What is it?

HILLCRIST. Hypocrite!

> [JILL *comes running in at the window.*

JILL. Dodo, she's moved; she's spoken.   It may not be so bad.

HILLCRIST. Thank God for that !   [FELLOWS *enters, Left.*

FELLOWS. The Jackmans, ma'am.

HILLCRIST. Who?   What's this?

> [*The* JACKMANS *have entered, standing close to the door.*

MRS. J. We're so glad we can go back, sir—ma'am, we just wanted to thank you.

> [*There is a silence, they see that they are not welcome.*]

Thank you kindly, sir.   Good-night, ma'am.

> [*They shuffle out.*

HILLCRIST. I'd forgotten their existence. [*He gets up.*] What is it that gets loose when you begin a fight, and makes you what you think you're not?   What blinding evil!   Begin as you may, it ends in this—skin game !   Skin game !

JILL. [*Rushing to him*] It's not you, Dodo; it's not you, beloved Dodo.

HILLCRIST. It is me.   For I am, or should be, master in this house.

MRS. H. I don't understand.

HILLCRIST. When we began this fight, we had clean hands —are they clean now?   What's gentility worth if it can't stand fire?

The curtain falls.

Made and printed in France.
7483-4-43. — Imp. CRÉTÉ, Corbeil. — C. O. L. 31-1631

A List of Pan Books

Lost Horizon — JAMES HILTON
Famous best-seller about strange adventures in a hidden corner of Tibet; unsurpassed for dreamlike excitement.

Random Harvest — JAMES HILTON
Skilful novel of suspense about successful business-man in whose memory there is a gap due to a war injury. By the author of *Lost Horizon*.

Ten Little Niggers — AGATHA CHRISTIE
The "ace of crime-novelists" tells of a series of murders when ten men and women (each with "a past") are invited to an island-mansion by an unknown host.

Towards Zero — AGATHA CHRISTIE
Brilliant detective novel showing how murder comes at the end of a series of events converging "towards zero".

Fire over England — A. E. W. MASON
Historical romance of secret service in the England of Queen Elizabeth and the Spain of the Armada.

The Four Million — O. HENRY
Twenty-five stories by one of the world's greatest masters in this field, whose work began to be published while he was in prison; with a special Introduction.

The Thirty-nine Steps — JOHN BUCHAN
World-renowned novel of adventure in London and Scotland leading to the foiling of an international plot.

Greenmantle — JOHN BUCHAN
Richard Hannay, hero of *The Thirty-nine Steps*, goes on a dangerous mission to find the mysterious "prophet" who plans to rouse the East against Britain.

The Man who Watched the Trains Go By — GEORGES SIMENON
Remarkable study of a quiet chess-playing Dutchman who becomes a murderer.

Burmese Silver — EDWARD THOMPSON

Adventure-tale of a fantastic English Raja in Burma, by author of high distinction as novelist, and poet.

These Foolish Things — MICHAEL SADLEIR

Romantic yet sophisticated novel by the author of *Fanny by Gaslight*, telling of a young man's education in love through disillusion and cynicism.

The Small Back Room — NIGEL BALCHIN

Swift, exciting tale of secret research-group of scientists in wartime as seen by a sensitive man who believes himself a failure, yet tackles a terrifying task.

Staying with Relations — ROSE MACAULAY

Entertaining novel about a young woman writer's visit to relatives living in a Central American forest. By author of *Potterism*, *Told by an Idiot*, etc.

Alive - Alive Oh ! — OSBERT SITWELL

Five long stories (from *Triple Fugue* and *Dumb Animal*) by winner of the *Sunday Times* £1,000 award for Literature in 1947.

The Enchanted April — "ELIZABETH"

Refreshing and humorous tale of four unhappy London ladies who find the solution of their problems under the spell of an Italian castle's spring beauty.

The Black Spectacles — JOHN DICKSON CARR

Ingenious detective-story based on a murder by poisoning in full view of three persons, not one of whom can afterwards describe accurately what happened.

The Lodger — MRS BELLOC LOWNDES

Famous novel (three times filmed) about the strange guest at a London lodging-house who is suspected of being responsible for a series of gruesome murders.

Goodbye to Murder — DONALD HENDERSON

Unusual, tensely told crime study of a woman with a curious liking for cushions, who finds murder necessary in her search for happiness.

Tales of the Supernatural

Eight tales from the literature of a hundred years. Bulwer Lytton, Maupassant, Pushkin, Tom Hood and R. L. Stevenson represent the 19th century, and M. R. James, Walter de la Mare and Hugh Walpole the modern masters.

Grand Hotel VICKI BAUM

Best-seller whose spectacular success as a book was followed by its even greater success as a film.

Journey without Maps GRAHAM GREENE

The provocative record of his journey on foot through the almost unexplored forests of the West African black republic of Liberia, by the author of *Brighton Rock*, *The Man Within*, etc. With a new Introduction.

The Stars are Dark PETER CHEYNEY

A galloping thriller of the Secret Service and counter-espionage by Britain's best-selling author.

The Matriarch G. B. STERN

Dedicated to John Galsworthy, this richly wov en novel of a Jewish family has achieved renown for its remarkable picture of a dominating but lovable woman.

Hostages to Fortune
ELIZABETH CAMBRIDGE

Novel of great charm, describing with quiet humour and realism middle-class family life from the point of view of a country doctor's wife with three children.

The Poor Man STELLA BENSON

Bitingly witty story set in California and China, by a short-lived writer whose exquisite work is of permanent value in British literature.

Death Comes to Cambers E. R. PUNSHON

Fine detective-story by a well-known author. Dorothy L. Sayers wrote: "In the works of Mr. E. R. Punshon we salute distinction every time."

The Suicide Club R. L. STEVENSON

Two sets of stories about the fantastic adventures of Prince Florizel (*The Suicide Club* and *The Rajah's Diamond*) in London and Paris.

Malice Aforethought — FRANCIS ILES

Superb study of a country doctor who turns murderer, which set a new fashion in crime-novels.

Hot Countries — ALEC WAUGH

Absorbing narrative of a series of journeys in the Far East, the West Indies and the South Sea Islands, when the author was a young novelist seeking colour, and adventure.

The Ringer — EDGAR WALLACE

As book, play, and film, this is one of its famous author's best thrillers, keeping the reader agog with excitement.

Trader Horn — ALOYSIUS HORN

« A gorgeous book, » writes John Galsworthy in the Fore-word to this racy record of adventures with cannibals, elephants and slavers (and the rescue of a white girl held by a native tribe) in West Africa in the seventies.

Yeoman's Hospital — HELEN ASHTON

Engrossing novel of 24 hours in the life of a hospital in an English country town, portraying the doctors, nurses, patients and domestic staff.

No Other Tiger — A. E. W. MASON

Admirable thriller, telling how a native murdered in the Burmese jungle is linked with happenings in England.

Pilgrim Cottage — CECIL ROBERTS

Romance of ballet-dancer and dramatist, with exciting scenes in Russia.

Mr. Perrin and Mr. Traill — HUGH WALPOLE

Renowned novel of conflict between two school-masters, played out to a violent end on the Cornish cliffs. Screened 1948 by Two Cities Films with Marius Goring, David Farrar and Greta Gynt.

The Mowgli Stories — RUDYARD KIPLING

Never before available at so low a price. Will be in great demand by members of the Boy Scout organisations.

Great Pan Double-Volumes

Alice's Adventures in Wonderland *with* Through the Looking-Glass   LEWIS CARROLL

Including all Sir John Tenniel's original 92 illustrations.

The Fountain   CHARLES MORGAN

Distinguished love-story, pitched on a high spiritual level, which has achieved international fame.

Fanny by Gaslight   MICHAEL SADLEIR

Famous novel about a girl brought up in the coarse and brutal underworld of the high society of London in the 1870's, by author whose knowledge of the period is unrivalled.

Guide to Modern Thought   C. E. M. JOAD

By world-famous philosopher, this enlarged edition of a unique book surveys in easy to read language the latest developments in physics, biology, psychology, psycho-analysis, psychical research and much else.

The Years   VIRGINIA WOOLF

By the greatest English woman writer of our time, this novel depicts the 50 years from the eighteen-eighties to the nineteen-thirties, as seen through the everyday life of the members of a London family.

Royal Dukes   ROGER FULFORD

Highly entertaining biography of Queen Victoria's father and "wicked uncles"—the eccentric sons of George III whose lives used to be considered so scandalous that a curtain of modesty was drawn across their history.

The Young Melbourne   LORD DAVID CECIL

Fascinating biography of William Lamb (who as Lord Melbourne was to become Queen Victoria's famous Prime Minister) and of his wife's extraordinary love-affair with Byron. With 7 plates.